TYPO3 Extension Development

Developer's guide to creating feature-rich extensions using the TYPO3 API

Dmitry Dulepov

BIRMINGHAM - MUMBAI

TYPO3 Extension Development

First published: September 2008

Production Reference: 1190908

Published by Packt Publishing Ltd.
32 Lincoln Road
Olton
Birmingham, B27 6PA, UK.

ISBN 978-1-847192-12-7

www.packtpub.com

Cover Image by Vinayak Chittar (vinayak.chittar@gmail.com)

Credits

Author

Dmitry Dulepov

Reviewer

Ingo Renner

Acquisition Editor

Adil Ahmed

Development Editor

Nikhil Bangera

Technical Editor

Dhiraj Bellani

Copy Editor

Sumathi Sridhar

Editorial Team Leader

Mithil Kulkarni

Project Manager

Abhijeet Deobhakta

Project Coordinator

Rajashree Hamine

Indexers

Rekha Nair

Monica Ajmera

Proofreader

Angie Butcher

Production Coordinators

Aparna Bhagat

Rajni Thorat

Cover Designer

Aparna Bhagat

About the Author

Dmitry Dulepov is a TYPO3 core team member and developer of several popular extensions (such as RealURL, TemplaVoila, comments, ratings, and others). He is known by his active support of the TYPO3 community through TYPO3 mailing lists. In 2008 Dmitry won the contest to appear on the first TYPO3 playing cards. He runs a popular blog where he regularly publishes original tips and articles about various TYPO3 features. In addition to his continuous TYPO3 core and extension development, Dmitry provides support for the TYPO3 translation team on behalf of the core team.

The author would like to thank everyone who helped with the book. This includes but is not limited to:

- Packt Publishing, for their very prompt answering of every question and giving helpful comments.

- Ingo Renner, who reviewed the book and made really good additions, notes, and corrections.

- My colleagues from Netcreators BV, especially to Ben van 't Ende, who always said that the book is important and Michiel Roos, who gave me some ideas during our work together on a TYPO3 project.

- My wife and kids, who understood the importance of this work and supported me in this work; my cats, who reminded me to make breaks and stretch by jumping on my knees in the least expected moments.

- To the TYPO3 community, who helped me to understand typically met issues with TYPO3 extension development.

The author is sure that the book will be useful to the reader and hopes to see more great extensions from the readers of the book soon.

About the Reviewer

Ingo Renner has been active in the TYPO3 project for about five years now. He started contributing to the project with a table-less template for the popular news extension "tt_news". Since then he has been active in many other areas including the content rendering group, digital asset management project, and the core team. Besides that, he's also known as a co-development leader for tt_news, current maintainer of tt_address, and lead developer for TYPO3's blog extension TIMTAB. In 2007, he joined the core team and was suddenly charged with the role of the release manager for TYPO3 4.2 - TYPO3's recent release. In March 2008, he graduated from the University of Applied Sciences, Darmstadt, with a Master of Science in Computer Science.

Ingo is a freelancer specialized in TYPO3 core development and always looking for interesting projects to improve the TYPO3 core.

Table of Contents

Preface

This is the first book in English to cover TYPO3 extension development in detail. The author is a member of the TYPO3 core team and developer of many popular TYPO3 extensions. Both novice and experienced TYPO3 programmers can use this book to build the extension they need following best practices and saving a lot of time that would otherwise have been spent pouring though the documentation.

The book is structured so that following the chapters in order builds a TYPO3 extension from the ground up. Experienced developers can use individual chapters independently to get only the information that they need.

Each chapter is divided so that the first part contains a description and discussion of the topic covered followed by a coding example with an explanation of how principles and techniques from the first part are followed in the code.

The reader is encouraged not only to read the book but also to look into the discussed classes and actually code the extension while reading the book.

What This Book Covers

Chapter 1 gives an overview of the TYPO3 API and tells about the most important classes in TYPO3.

Chapter 2 describes files in the TYPO3 extension, what role they play and how to use them.

Chapter 3 focuses on planning. Planning makes extensions better. It makes the project successful.

Chapter 4 walks the reader through the process of extension generation. All options are explained, several issues are pointed out, and useful tips provided.

Chapter 5 focuses on the Frontend plugin theory. It also provides a lot of tips to make extensions effective.

Chapter 6 is dedicated to practical progamming. The reader will see how to make list, search, and single views, use AJAX from the Frontend plugin, and create useful TypoScript for the plugin.

Chapter 7 focuses on the Backend module programming.

Chapter 8 describes how to write documentation for the extension and polish the code before releasing it to TER.

What You Need for This Book

The author assumes that the reader has the following knowledge:

- PHP programming
  The reader is expected to have some experience with PHP and knowledge about PHP classes in general. No prior TYPO3 programming experience is needed.

- TYPO3 as an administrator
  Basic knowledge of TYPO3, TypoScript, and TYPO3 extension idea.

- TYPO3 documentation
  The reader should know what is TSRef, TSConfig, **TYPO3 Core API**. The reader should be able to find these documents in the **Documentation** section of the `http://typo3.org/` website.

- Basic knowledge about phpDoc.

Who is This Book For

This book is for PHP developers who want to develop a TYPO3 extension. It assumes the reader has experience with PHP, XML, and HTML. No prior knowledge about TYPO3 extension programming or the TYPO3 API is presumed.

Conventions

In this book, you will find a number of styles of text that distinguish between different kinds of information. Here are some examples of these styles, and an explanation of their meaning.

Code words in text are shown as follows: " Notice how `param1` is passed as a value first and then as an array by using a dot."

A block of code will be set as follows:

```
plugin.tx_myext_pi1 = USER
plugin.tx_myext_pi1 {
    userFunc = tx_myext_pi1->main
}
```

When we wish to draw your attention to a particular part of a code block, the relevant lines or items will be made bold:

```
plugin.tx_myext_pi1 = USER
plugin.tx_myext_pi1 {
    includeLibs = EXT:myext/pi1/class.tx_myext_pi1.php
    userFunc = tx_myext_pi1->main
}
```

New terms and **important words** are introduced in a bold-type font. Words that you see on the screen, in menus or dialog boxes for example, appear in our text like this: "To finish this step, press the **Update...** button".

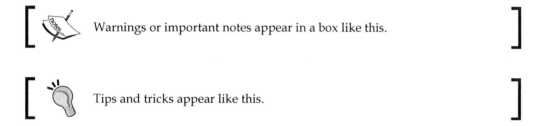

Warnings or important notes appear in a box like this.

Tips and tricks appear like this.

Reader Feedback

Feedback from our readers is always welcome. Let us know what you think about this book, what you liked or may have disliked. Reader feedback is important for us to develop titles that you really get the most out of.

To send us general feedback, simply drop an email to feedback@packtpub.com, making sure to mention the book title in the subject of your message.

If there is a book that you need and would like to see us publish, please send us a note in the **SUGGEST A TITLE** form on www.packtpub.com or email suggest@packtpub.com.

If there is a topic that you have expertise in and you are interested in either writing or contributing to a book, see our author guide on www.packtpub.com/authors.

Customer Support

Now that you are the proud owner of a Packt book, we have a number of things to help you to get the most from your purchase.

Downloading the Example Code for the Book

Visit http://www.packtpub.com/files/code/2127_Code.zip to directly download the example code.

[The downloadable files contain instructions on how to use them.]

Errata

Although we have taken every care to ensure the accuracy of our contents, mistakes do happen. If you find a mistake in one of our books — maybe a mistake in text or code — we would be grateful if you would report this to us. By doing this you can save other readers from frustration, and help to improve subsequent versions of this book. If you find any errata, report them by visiting http://www.packtpub.com/support, selecting your book, clicking on the **let us know** link, and entering the details of your errata. Once your errata are verified, your submission will be accepted and the errata added to the list of existing errata. The existing errata can be viewed by selecting your title from http://www.packtpub.com/support.

Piracy

Piracy of copyright material on the Internet is an ongoing problem across all media. At Packt, we take the protection of our copyright and licenses very seriously. If you come across any illegal copies of our works in any form on the Internet, please provide the location address or website name immediately so we can pursue a remedy.

Please contact us at copyright@packtpub.com with a link to the suspected pirated material.

We appreciate your help in protecting our authors, and our ability to bring you valuable content.

Questions

You can contact us at questions@packtpub.com if you are having a problem with some aspect of the book, and we will do our best to address it.

1
About TYPO3 API

Let's get a picture of TYPO3 API before we start to talk about extension creation. There are a lot of files, functions, and function groups in TYPO3 API. Beginners can easily miss the function they should use in a particular part of the code.

This chapter is going to discuss TYPO3 API. We will not go into the details, but will provide pointers to where developers can look. The best way to read this chapter is to keep a copy of each discussed PHP file and read function description inside that file along with the description mentioned in the book.

After completing this chapter, the reader will have a general picture of TYPO3 API, and will be able to find the necessary functions in the API.

Overview of TYPO3 API

TYPO3 is a large system with lots of PHP classes. Trying to learn each class in order to learn the API is time consuming, and will not provide an understanding of the system as a whole. It is much easier to logically split the system into blocks and look at the API from this perspective.

As seen from the user experience, TYPO3 has two main parts: the Frontend (or FE) and the Backend (or BE). Website visitors see the FE of TYPO3. Website editors create and modify the website content from the BE of TYPO3.

The TYPO3 API can be divided approximately the same way: FE API and BE API. The FE API includes classes to create website output, while the BE API includes classes for content manipulation and other functionality to help editors do their work in an effective way. Extensions can extend existing or add new APIs to the system. One of the best examples is TemplaVoila. It adds point-and-click templates to the TYPO3 BE and flexible content elements to the FE.

However, there is one more part, which is not visible to website visitors or editors but used by both FE and BE API. There is no name for it in TYPO3. In this book, we will call it the Common API. An example of such an API is the database API. It would be wrong to use different database layers for BE and FE (otherwise programmers would have to learn more APIs and would tend to use the one most convenient instead of the one "assigned" to Backend or Frontend). So, TYPO3 has only one layer that works with the database. All system classes and extensions are expected to use this API to access and retrieve data from the database.

While we can logically separate the TYPO3 API into three parts, it should be noted that most TYPO3 classes and functions have a very long history. They are constantly updated, but their age is still visible. Most classes are in the same file system directory (t3lib), and it is hard to tell where the class really belongs just by looking at its name. However, this applies only to the file system. Generally, these classes include functions for a single API group only. So logically, they are well-designed and separated from other groups.

The TYPO3 core team makes every effort to keep the API clear, logical, and effective. Extension developers can learn a lot about TYPO3 by looking into the implementation of the TYPO3 API while programming extensions. This is really a good way to become a TYPO3 professional.

In the following sections, we will look at each API group and certain classes inside them. Due to the large number of API classes, it is not possible to cover them all. It would take the whole book alone to cover them all. So, we are going to cover only those classes that extension developers will most likely meet or use during extension development. We are going to start with the most basic and universal classes and move on to more specialized classes. Note that this chapter will provide only an overview of the API, and not a detailed description of each function. We will look deeper into many of these classes later in the book.

But first, we need to discuss certain basic issues about TYPO3 from a developer's view.

PHP Classes and Files

There are certain conventions concerning file and class naming in TYPO3. They must be used in extensions too and knowing these conventions helps to locate files quickly.

Each class file starts with `class.` and is followed by a class name in lower case. The file ends with a `.php` extension. There are certain exceptions to this rule, and they will be described in this book. These exceptions exist due to historical reasons, and no new class may become an exception.

Classes have a certain prefix that declares where they belong in the TYPO3 class hierarchy. The following system prefixes are defined:

- t3lib_
- tslib_
- tx_
- ux_
- user_

Each prefix corresponds to a "library" if it ends with "lib_", and to a "namespace" otherwise. "Library" is just a way to say that a "namespace" belongs to TYPO3. In other words, library classes are TYPO3 classes. Extensions cannot introduce new library classes.

t3lib_

t3lib stands for "TYPO3 library". This name is historical, and everyone just calls it t3lib (tee-three-lib). t3lib is the largest collection of classes in TYPO3. It includes most Common, FE, and BE classes. It is easy to say that a class belongs to t3lib by looking at its name. Here are some examples:

- `t3lib_DB`
- `t3lib_div`
- `t3lib_TCEmain`

We will look at some t3lib classes later in this chapter.

tslib_

tslib stands for "TypoScript Library", The name has historical reasons as well and everyone calls this library tslib (tee-es-lib). It is located in the `typo3/sysext/cms/tslib` directory (inside the `cms` system extension). Most of these classes are already included when code runs in FE. So there is no need to include them explicitly in extensions.

The library classes are responsible for the rendering of the website and most of the FE logic. The base class for FE plugins (modules that extend TYPO3 Frontend functionality) is also located here.

We will discuss tslib classes in the **Frontend API** section.

Here is a list of some classes in tslib:

- `tslib_fe`
  This is the main FE class in TYPO3. It represents a page that a website visitor sees in the browser. There is only one instance of this class in TYPO3 FE, and it is available as and generally referred as "TSFE".

- `tslib_cobj`
  This is one of the exclusions to generic naming rule mentioned earlier. This class is located in the file named `class.tslib_content.php`, but the class name is different. This class implements **content objects**. Content objects is a TYPO3 way of generating different types of content. There are many content objects, for example, TEXT, IMAGE, or HMENU. They are the same content objects as found in TypoScript. FE plugins from extensions are USER or USER_INT content objects. Instances of this class can either be created directly (see later in this chapter), or by calling .

- `tslib_fetce`
  This is an attempt to bring some BE functions (such as `clear_cacheCmd`) to the FE. While this class exists, it is not really updated and should not be used.

- `tslib_feuserauth`
  This is an internal class that authenticates website visitors ("Frontend users"). This class is created and used by TSFE. An instance of this class is always available as .

- `tslib_pibase`
  This is a base class for FE plugins. We will cover it in detail in Chapter 5.

tx_

This namespace is reserved for extensions ("tx" stands for "TYPO3 Extensions"). All extension classes must begin with `tx_` (with the exception of "ux" classes).

ux_

This namespace is reserved for XCLASSes. XCLASS is a way to subclass a class in TYPO3 and make use of the subclass instead of the parent class in a way that is transparent to all the other classes in the system. Normally, XCLASSes are provided by extensions. XCLASSes take the class and file name of the parent class but prepend it with `ux_`, as in `class.ux_tslib_fe.php` or `class.ux_t3lib_tcemain.php`.

While XCLASSes may seem the easiest way to modify system behavior, they should be avoided and used only if there is absolutely no other way to change system behavior. The fundamental limitations of XCLASSes is that there can be only one XCLASS for a given class in the system. If two extensions try to XCLASS the same class, only the last one will succeed.

user_

This namespace is reserved for PHP functions outside of a class. TYPO3 will refuse to call any function outside of a class that is not prefixed with user_. If an extension key has this prefix, it means that the extension is private. Such extensions cannot be sent to the TYPO3 Extension Repository. Typically, such extensions are created for testing purposes.

How Data Is Stored in TYPO3

TYPO3 uses a database (typically MySQL) and the file system to store data. The file system keeps configuration files, some cache files, images, and uploaded files. The database stores pages, content elements, and lots of system data (such as TypoScript templates, logs, and so on).

All (to be precise most, but for our purpose, all) tables in TYPO3 roughly follow the same structure. They have a set of predefined (reserved) fields. TYPO3 will not work properly if one or more of the required fields is missing. Examples of predefined fields are uid (unique identifier of the record), pid (id of the page where this record is located), crdate (record creation time), tstamp (last update time), cruser_id (uid of the Backend user, who created this record). A table may also contain other reserved fields. If it does, TYPO3 will automatically provide additional functionality for the table. The best examples of such fields are deleted (indicates whether a record is deleted), starttime (indicates when a record becomes visible in the FE), endtime (indicates when a record stops being visible), and hidden (indicates whether a record is hidden). There are other fields, which will be discussed later. All these fields are managed by the system, and extensions usually do not change them.

TYPO3 comes with several default tables. These main tables are:

- pages and pages_language_overlay
  The pages table stores page data (uid, title, and so on), while the pages_language_overlay table stores translations of the page data.
- tt_content
  This table stores information about content elements. This is usually one of the largest tables in the system.

- `be_*`
  This table stores information related to BE users.
- `cache_*`
  This table stores cache data.
- `fe_*`
  This table stores information related to FE users.
- `sys_*`
  This tables stores various system data.
- `tx_*`
  This table stores tables from extensions.

If an extension provides a new table, it must ensure that the table name has a certain format. The table name must start with `tx_`, followed first by the extension key without underscores and next by an underscore, and the table name. For example, an extension with the extension key `my_ext` can have the following valid table names:

- `tx_myext_data`
- `tx_myext_elements`

The following table names are not valid:

- `data`
- `myext_data`
- `my_ext_data`
- `data_my_ext`
- `tx_my_ext_data`

We will discuss tables in more detail when we generate extensions later in this book. At the moment, it is important to remember two things:

- There are certain naming conventions for tables.
- Each table must have a certain set of fields.

Common TYPO3 API

As explained earlier, all TYPO3 API functions can be divided into three groups. The Common API group contains classes that are common in the other two groups, FE and BE API. These classes are essential for extension developers because they are either "most used" or "most must-be-used". We will examine these classes in the later sections. Since this chapter is called "About TYPO3 API", its purpose is to provide an overview, and not a fully detailed description. You can use this chapter as a guideline and learn more by looking at the source code of the discussed classes.

Database API

Database API is the most independent class of all the TYPO3 API classes. It contains functions to manipulate data in the MySQL database. The class name is t3lib_DB. There is no TYPO3-specific functionality, only a set of convenient methods to access the database. The instance of this class is available, both in FE and BE, as $GLOBALS['TYPO3_DB'].

All core classes and all extensions must work with the TYPO3 database by using t3lib_DB. This ensures that the database is accessed correctly. Using MySQL PHP functions directly is strongly discouraged and may, in certain cases, interfere with TYPO3 database access, or even break the TYPO3 database.

Besides convenient methods, t3lib_DB has another purpose. Since this is an API class, it can be XCLASSed to provide access to other databases transparent to the rest of TYPO3. This is what the extension DBAL does.

Here is an example of how the TYPO3 database can be accessed using t3lib_DB:

```
// Select number of non-deleted pages
$res = $GLOBALS['TYPO3_DB']->exec_SELECTquery(
        'COUNT(*) AS t', 'pages',
        'deleted=0');
if ($res !== false) {
    // Fetch array with data
    $row = $GLOBALS['TYPO3_DB']->sql_fetch_assoc($res);
    if ($row !== false) {
        $numberOfDeletedPages = $row['t'];
    }
    // Free resultset (or memory leak will happen)
    $GLOBALS['TYPO3_DB']->sql_free_result($res);
}
```

As you can see, these functions look very similar to MySQL PHP functions. This similarity is not accidental. The default database for TYPO3 is MySQL, and the database API is modeled using MySQL PHP functions.

Generally, all functions can be divided into several groups.

The first group consists of functions that generate various SQL queries. Functions accept certain parameters (such as field names, table name, SQL WHERE condition, and so on) and return a properly constructed SQL query. This is good for extensions that need compatibility with different database types. However, it should be noted that these functions cannot always be used, especially if the query is complex, such as with SQL JOIN constructs, and so on. Functions in this group are:

- `function INSERTquery($table,array $fields_values, $no_quote_fields=FALSE)`

- ```
  function UPDATEquery($table,$where,array $fields_values,
  $no_quote_fields=FALSE)
  ```
- ```
  function DELETEquery($table,$where)
  ```
- ```
  function SELECTquery($select_fields,$from_table,$where_clause,$
  groupBy='',$orderBy='',$limit='')
  ```

The next group is similar to the first group. It consists of functions that build and execute queries. Most functions in this group are built around functions belonging to the first group. Here you may ask a question: why does the first group exist then? The answer is simple. Sometimes, you want to get a query first, log it somewhere, and then execute it. In that case, you may want to use functions from the first group.

Here is a list of functions from the second group:

- ```
  function exec_INSERTquery($table,array $fields_values,
  $no_quote_fields=FALSE)
  ```
- ```
  function exec_UPDATEquery($table,$where,array $fields_values,
  $no_quote_fields=FALSE)
  ```
- ```
  function exec_DELETEquery($table,$where)
  ```
- ```
  function exec_SELECTquery($select_fields,$from_table,$where_cla
  use,$groupBy='',$orderBy='',$limit='')
  ```
- ```
  function exec_SELECT_mm_query($select,$local_table,
  $mm_table,$foreign_table,$whereClause='',$groupBy='',
  $orderBy='',$limit='')
  ```
- ```
  function exec_SELECT_queryArray($queryParts)
  ```
- ```
  function exec_SELECTgetRows($select_fields,$from_table,$where_c
  lause,$groupBy='',$orderBy='',$limit='',$uidIndexField='')
  ```

The last three functions may raise questions. Two of them are rarely used. The `exec_SELECT_mm_query` function is a TYPO3 way to execute a query on tables with many-to-many relations. The `exec_SELECT_queryArray` function executes a SELECT SQL query, taking parameters from the passed array. This function is rarely used. The last one will perform a SELECT SQL query, fetch rows, and return them in an array. This function should be used with caution; if the result is big, it may exhaust PHP memory easily. But for some results, it is the most convenient way to fetch data from the database.

The next group includes functions to fetch the result, get the number of rows, and so on. They are identical to the corresponding MySQL PHP functions. They are so trivial that we will not discuss them much, only list them here for the sake of completeness:

- `function sql_query($query)`
- `function sql_error()`
- `function sql_num_rows($res)`
- `function sql_fetch_assoc($res)`
- `function sql_fetch_row($res)`
- `function sql_free_result($res)`
- `function sql_insert_id()`
- `function sql_affected_rows()`
- `function sql_data_seek($res,$seek)`
- `function sql_field_type($res,$pointer)`

One important note for extension authors: do not forget to call the `sql_free_result()` function! Though the PHP manual says that MySQL resources are automatically released when the script terminates, in practice, this does not always happen (especially, if persistent connections are enabled). Moreover, if DBAL is enabled, automatic freeing of resources may not always work. It is always better to clean them up in the code.

The last group of functions are the utility functions. While we are looking at it as the last group, functions in this group are used (or must be used) all the time. This group includes functions to escape database parameters and to do query manipulation. Here is a list:

- `function fullQuoteStr($str, $table)`
- `function fullQuoteArray($arr, $table, $noQuote=FALSE)`
- `function quoteStr($str, $table)`
- `function escapeStrForLike($str, $table)`
- `function cleanIntArray($arr)`
- `function cleanIntList($list)`
- `function stripOrderBy($str)`
- `function stripGroupBy($str)`
- `function splitGroupOrderLimit($str)`
- `function listQuery($field, $value, $table)`
- `function listQuery($searchWords, $fields, $table)`

The `fullQuoteStr()` function is possibly the most used (or again – the most "must-be-used") function in this group. It escapes all special characters in the string and additionally wraps the string in quotes in a manner compatible with the current database. Therefore, extension developers should use this function for both escaping and quoting parameters, and not use any "home-made" solution. This is a good security-related function. Other functions do more or less the same but in more specialized way. The "strip" and "split" functions are specific for some TYPO3 core calls (but can be called by extensions too).

Now, we are ready to see more complex examples of database API functions. Notice that this example is focused on the database API only. You should not use this code in the extension because it lacks certain calls to other APIs, is not effective from the point of view of database performance, and uses `echo` (TYPO3 uses other ways of showing generated content). But this example gives a good idea of how to use the database API.

```
/**
 * Retrieves all news written by the given author
 *
 * @param string $authorName   Author name
 * @return       array  A list of news items for author
 */
function findNewsByAuthor($authorName) {
    $res = $GLOBALS['TYPO3_DB']->exec_SELECTquery('uid,title',
        'tt_news',
        'author=' .
        $GLOBALS['TYPO3_DB']->fullQuoteStr(
            $authorName, 'tt_news'));
    $news = array();
    while (false !==
        ($row = $GLOBALS['TYPO3_DB']->sql_fetch_assoc($res))) {
        $news[$row['uid']] = $row['title']
    }
    $GLOBALS['TYPO3_DB']->sql_free_result($res);
    return $news;
}
/**
 * Marks all news written by the given author as deleted
 *
 * @param string $authorName
 * @return       void
 */
function deleteNewsForAuthor($author) {
    $news = findNewsForAuthor($author);
    $fields = array('deleted' => 1);
    foreach ($news as $uid => $title) {
```

```
        echo 'Deleted news item with id=' . $uid . ' (' .
            $title . ')' . chr(10);
        $GLOBALS['TYPO3_DB']->UPDATEquery('tt_news',
            'uid=' . $GLOBALS['TYPO3_DB']->fullQuoteStr(
            $uid, 'tt_news'), $fields);
        if ($GLOBALS['TYPO3_DB']->sql_affected_rows() == 0) {
        echo 'The above news item was already deleted';
        }
    }
}
```

Extension Management

Extension management is a class with functions that provides various levels of information about extensions. This class is not to be confused with TYPO3 Extension Manager.

The Extension management class is named t3lib_extMgm. The functions that developers are likely to use are:

- function isLoaded($key,$exitOnError=0)
  Checks if an extension is loaded. Useful if the extension uses functionality of another extension.
- function extPath($key,$script='')
  Returns the absolute path to the script $script in the extension identified by $key. The $script variable contains a path relative to the extension directory. This can be used in the require_once PHP function.
- function extRelPath($key)
  Returns a path to the extension directory relative to the /typo3 directory. This can be used for <a>, <img>, <link>, or <script> tags to include the extension's files in Backend scripts.
- function siteRelPath($key)
  Returns a path to the extension directory relative to the site root. It is used for the same purpose as extRelPath, but in the FE.

Here are some code examples:

```
$extkey = 'templavoila';
require_once(t3lib_extMgm::extPath($extkey,
        'pi1/class.tx_templavoila_pi1.php'));
// From Backend:
$link = '<a href="' . t3lib_extMgm::extRelPath($extkey) .
        'mod1/index.php">Reload</a>';
// From Frontend
$link = '<img src="' . t3lib_extMgm::siteRelPath($extkey) .
        'res/image.gif" />';
```

There are also other functions to use form extensions, but we will discuss them in detail when we meet them because they have very specific usage.

Helper Functions (t3lib_div)

There is a class in TYPO3 that contains the largest collection of various public functions (138 at the time of writing). This class is probably the most used one in TYPO3. The class name is t3lib_div. It is located in t3lib/class.t3lib_div.php.

All functions in this class are divided into several groups. Most popular functions will be described in the forthcoming sections. They all need to be called statically (using t3lib_div::funcName() syntax). The t3lib_div function is always included and available in any extension. There is no need to include this file in your own scripts.

If you think you need a generic function, it is good to check if t3lib_div already has it, before writing your own.

GET/POST Functions

The Get and Post functions should be used in TYPO3 extensions to obtain values of request variables. While PHP contains variables such as $_GET and $_POST that can be used in scripts, TYPO3 coding guidelines require one to use TYPO3 functions to obtain values of request parameters. TYPO3 runs on many different web servers, and some of them have different ways of passing parameters to PHP scripts. Using TYPO3 functions ensures that the script always gets the parameter, regardless of the web server. The TYPO3 core team will fix the core if a new platform is found causing troubles with script parameters. This way extensions become independent of the differences in web server implementation. Extension authors can concentrate on their code instead of making workarounds for web servers.

The following functions are defined:

- function _GP($var)

  This function retrieves the value from POST and, if not found, from GET request parameters.

- function _GET($var=NULL)

  Retrieves value from GET request parameter.

- function _POST($var=NULL)

  Retrieves value from POST request parameter.

- `function _GETset($inputGet,$key='')`

  Sets the value of GET request parameter. There is no equivalent for POST.

- `function GParrayMerged($var)`

  Many TYPO3 modules pass parameters in URLs as arrays. If PHP finds something like `tx_extkey_pi1[param]=123` in the URL, `tx_extkey_pi1` will be an array with a key named `param` and value, `123`. This function will merge such an array for POST and GET, with POST taking preference, and returning this array.

String Functions

There are several functions in this group that perform common tasks:

- `function fixed_lgd_cs($string,$chars)`

  This function will crop a string and append three dots to the string. The `$chars` variable indicates the length. If the value is negative, it will crop that amount of characters from the end of the string. This function will work well only if `$GLOBALS['LANG']` (see section about localization) is set. So it is generally limited to BE scripts usage.

- `function testInt($var)`

  This function checks if the passed variable is an integer. Variables in PHP can be freely converted between types. For example, `'2'+'3'` gives 5. This function will return `true` for 3 and `'3'`, but not for `'3x'`. Thus, it is very convenient to validate some parameters (like database identifiers).

- `function isFirstPartOfStr($str,$partStr)`

  The name of this function is self-explanatory.

- `function validEmail($email)`

  This function checks if the passed email has the correct syntax. It does not check whether that domain is valid or whether the mail account exists.

Array Functions

Array functions manipulate array data. Here is the list of the most useful functions:

- `function implodeArrayForUrl($name,$theArray,$str='',$skipBlank=0, $rawurlencodeParamName=0)`

  This function creates a URL query string from the passed array. Keys become parameter names, values become parameter values. If `$name` is not empty, each parameter becomes a value in the array with this name (see description of `GParrayMerged` above). The `$str` variable must be blank (TYPO3 uses it internally when calling this function recursively).

- function array_merge_recursive_overrule($arr0,$arr1,$notAddKeys=0, $includeEmtpyValues=true)
  This function recursively merges two arrays. The second array overrides the first. If $notAddKeys is set, key/value pairs from the second array are ignored if the corresponding key does not exist in the first array.

- function csvValues($row,$delim=',',$quote='"')
  Creates a comma-separated string of values and takes care of new line characters. The result can be imported into a spreadsheet application. Note that it works on a single row of data and should be called as many times as there are rows. Useful for dumping data into CSV files.

XML Processing

There are only two very specific functions that we will mention here. They are used to convert XML to a PHP array, and vice versa.

- function array2xml($array,$NSprefix='',$level=0,$docTag='phparray', $spaceInd=0, $options=array(),$stackData=array())
  This function converts a PHP array into XML. We will not describe it in detail here. but recommend that you refer to the documentation inside this function to see all possible options (there are too many of them).

- function xml2array($string,$NSprefix='',$reportDocTag=FALSE)
  Converts an XML string into an array.

Before using these functions, you should remember that PHP arrays cannot have multiple values with the same key. So, if there are repeating nodes in your XML, you have to add an attribute named index to them. This attribute becomes a key. Here is an example:

```
<data>
    <node index="1"><value>value 1</value></node>
    <node index="2"><value>value 2</value></node>
    <node index="3"><value>value 3</value></node>
</data>
```

Running xml2array produces the following PHP array:

```
Array
(
    [1] => Array
        (
            [value] => value 1
        )
    [2] => Array
        (
```

```
                [value] => value 2
            )
    [3] => Array
        (
                [value] => value 3
        )
)
```

Without the `index` attribute, the array becomes:

```
Array
(
    [node] => Array
        (
                [value] => value 3
        )
)
```

File, Directory, and URL Functions

These functions perform the most common tasks for file, directory, and URLs. Here is the list:

- `function getURL($url, $includeHeader=0)`

  This function fetches a URL and returns the result. This function must be used instead of `fopen()` or `file_get_contents()` because PHP functions may be disabled by security settings on the server. However, `getURL` may use other methods to fetch the content of the URL.

- `function writeFileToTypo3tempDir($filepath,$content)`

  This function writes a file to the TYPO3 temporary directory.

- `function getFilesInDir($path,$extensionList='', $prependPath=0,$order='')`

- `function getAllFilesAndFoldersInPath($fileArr,$path, $extList='',$regDirs=0,$recursivityLevels=99)`

- `function fixWindowsFilePath($theFile)`

- `function locationHeaderUrl($path)`

  This function takes a path and returns a correct URL to be used for redirection using the `header()` PHP function.

Debug Functions

These functions dump passed variables. Note that the web IP address of website visitors must be included in the `devIPmask` parameter in the TYPO3 Install tool, so that these functions can be used for urgent debugging on a live site!

- `function print_array($array_in)`

- `function debug($var="",$brOrHeader=0)`

- `function debug_trail()`
  Returns stack trace with entries separated by `//`.

- `function debugRows($rows,$header='')`

System Functions

These are general-purpose functions. They do not fit into any other group. Therefore we list them here:

- `function getThisUrl()`

- `function linkThisScript($getParams=array())`
  Returns a link to this script. All the parameters are preserved. It is possible to override the parameters by passing an array with new name/value pairs.

- `function linkThisUrl($url,$getParams=array())`
  This function is similar to the previous function except that it returns a link to the URL.

- `function getIndpEnv($getEnvName)`
  This function is the way TYPO3 gets server variables such as `HTTP_HOST` or `REMOTE_ADDR`. TYPO3 runs on many platforms and under many web servers. Not all these servers return parameters in the same way. This function takes care of the differences, and will always return a server parameter, regardless of the server software. It must be used instead of `$_SERVER` and `$_ENV` PHP variables. In addition, this function can return values of TYPO3-defined variables. Here is a list of these variables:

    - `TYPO3_HOST_ONLY`
      Host name
    - `TYPO3_PORT`
      Port (blank if 80, taken from host value)
    - `TYPO3_REQUEST_HOST`
      [scheme]://[host][:[port]]
    - `TYPO3_REQUEST_URL`
      [scheme]://[host][:[port]][path]?[query]
    - `TYPO3_REQUEST_SCRIPT`
      [scheme]://[host][:[port]][path_script]

○ TYPO3_REQUEST_DIR
   [scheme]://[host][:[port]][path_dir]
○ TYPO3_SITE_URL
   [scheme]://[host][:[port]][path_dir] of the TYPO3 website
   Frontend
○ TYPO3_SITE_SCRIPT
   [script / Speaking URL] of the TYPO3 website
○ TYPO3_DOCUMENT_ROOT
   Absolute path of root of documents: TYPO3_DOCUMENT_
   ROOT.SCRIPT_NAME = SCRIPT_FILENAME (typically)
○ TYPO3_SSL
   Returns TRUE if this session uses SSL/TLS (https)

TYPO3-Specific Functions

There are a lot of functions here that also fall into categories we have already seen. However, the functions discussed earlier are universal. They do not depend on TYPO3 variables and can generally be reused outside TYPO3. Functions from this group take TYPO3 into account. There are lots of them. We list only the ones that are likely to be used in extensions:

- function validPathStr($theFile)

- function tempnam($filePrefix)

  Creates a temporary file in the typo3temp/ directory.

- function loadTCA($table)

  Loads the table configuration array (TCA). We will discuss the TCA later in this book.

- function callUserFunction($funcName,&$params,&$ref, $checkPrefix='user_',$silent=0)

  Calls the user function. The function name has a certain format (see "TYPO3 File References" section that follows).

- function &getUserObj($classRef,$checkPrefix='user_',$silent=0)

  Instantiates a class and returns its instance.

- function &makeInstance($className)

  Creates an instance of the class, given its name. This function must be used instead of the new PHP operator. It takes care of proper XCLASS handling. Use this function even for your internal classes!

- function makeInstanceClassName($className)

  Checks if XCLASS is available for any given class and returns either the class or XCLASS name. It is useful when instantiating an object with parameters for the constructor. For example, function devLog($msg, $extKey, $severity=0, $dataVar=FALSE) logs messages to the developer log. By default, it does nothing. Requires logging extension (such as cc_devlog or rlmp_filedevlog) and SYS_DLOG enabled in TYPO3 Install tool. It is useful in recording a sequence of events on a production server. Beware of performance decline!

TYPO3 File References

TYPO3 has a special syntax to refer files or classes and functions inside files. Typically, it is used for extensions. This syntax is similar to a URL. Check the following code fragment:

```
$params = array();
$result = t3lib_div::callUserFunction(
    'EXT:myext/subdir/class.tx_myext_class.php:' .
    'tx_myext_class->main', $params, $this);
```

The callUserFunction function will read the function name as follows:

- EXT means that the function has an extension.
- Extension key follows the EXT: prefix until the first slash.
- Everything until the colon is the file path.
- If there is a -> sequence, then the function is a method of the class. The class will be instantiated using t3lib_div::makeInstance() and a method of the class will be called. The class name must start with tx_ or ux_ or user_. If there is no -> sequence, then it is a function without a class, and its name must start with user_. If the class or function name does not start with a proper prefix, then callUserFunction will refuse to call them.

The getUserObj function is similar to the callUserFunction function except that it does not have a function part, but a class name. It returns a class instance and the extension can call methods of this class. Name restrictions apply to getUserObj as well.

Language Support

TYPO3 supports many languages and works very well with them. It has a set of functions and classes that provide access to localized (translated) strings. These strings are stored in XML files. Extensions need not care about finding the right language or parsing XML because TYPO3 has a very good API for it. While using this API, all strings from XML can be referenced by their index. The index is also a string, but it stays non-localized. A string changes, but its index does not. So it is always possible to find the value of the string by its index. To give a short example, the "Click here" string may have a "click_here" index (the code example at the end of this section will make it clearer).

Usually, localization is one of the areas that lacks a developer's attention. It is much easier to hard-code strings in the PHP code than to write them to an XML file and add an extra line to load that string. But supporting translations is one thing that makes a good extension. Do not postpone the creation of language files. Do it properly from the beginning; do not hard-code. Write a string to an XML file and use the API to get its value.

What happens if an extension is not translated to another language (partially or fully)? The labels in the default language (English) will be used instead.

The class that implements localization support for strings is an old class and, as many old classes, it is an exception to the naming rule described earlier in this chapter. The class name is `language` and it is located in `typo3/sysext/lang` (system extension `lang`). In the BE, it is usually available as `$GLOBALS['LANG']`. In the FE, it is not available directly, but there are similar ways to get localized strings.

The following methods are the most used ones:

- `function init($lang,$altPath='')`

  This function initializes the `language` class for the given language code. Languge code is TYPO3-specific. The special code value `default` refers to the English language. You will rarely need to use this function. Generally, it is enough to know that you have to call this function if for any reason you need to create an instance of the `language` class yourself. But if you really have to, it means that you are doing something nontrivial, and you should be an experienced extension writer to use this function.

- `function getLL($index,$hsc=0)`

  This function returns a label by its string index. Labels must be included using the `includeLLFile` function (see below).

- function getLLL($index,$LOCAL_LANG,$hsc=0)

  Does the same as getLL, but uses the $LOCAL_LANG argument to search for the string.

- function sL($input,$hsc=0)

  This function is the most complex but also the most powerful among all the functions in this class. It accepts string reference in a special format and returns the string. The string reference format is similar to the format described earlier in the section named "TYPO3 File References", but it must be prepended with the LLL: prefix, for example, LLL:EXT:lang/local-lang_general.xml:LGL.image. This reference tells TYPO3 to load a string identified by LGL.image index from the file named locallang_general.xml in lang extension. The $hsc parameter allows automatic application of the htmlspecialchars PHP function to the returned string.

- function includeLLFile($fileRef,$setGlobal=1, $mergeLocalOntoDefault=0)

  This function loads information from a language file into a global variable for use with the getLL function. It accepts EXT: file referencing format for files as well as the absolute path.

- function readLLfile($fileRef)

  This function reads a language file and returns labels for the current language to the caller. It also accepts the EXT: syntax for $fileRef.

Here is a full code example:

```
require_once(t3lib_extMgm::extPath('lang', 'lang.php'));
$lang = t3lib_div::makeInstance('language');
/* @var $lang language */
$lang->init('default');
$fileRef = 'EXT:lang/locallang_general.xml';
$label1 = $lang->sL('LLL:' . $fileRef . ':LGL.image');
$LL = $lang->readLLfile($fileRef);
$label2 = $lang->getLLL('LGL.image', $LL);
$lang->includeLLFile($fileRef);
$label3 = $lang->getLL('LGL.image');
```

All three labels are identical in this example.

Reference Index

TYPO3 stores data in the database. Often, data records refer to other data records or files in the file system. If a data record is deleted and it has a reference to a file, the file stays in the file system. If another data record refers to the deleted data record, there will be a dead link.

To prevent these kinds of problems, TYPO3 maintains a separate list of references between data records and files in the system. This is called the "reference index". The class name is `t3lib_refindex`.

When data records are created, modified, or deleted in Backend using TCEmain (described in the **Backend API** section below), the system will update the reference index automatically. FE is different; TCEmain does not work there. FE plugins usually insert data directly into the database using the database API described earlier in this book. So, extension developers have to take care and update the reference index manually. Unfortunately, very few extensions do. Originally, the reference index was developed for BE usage, but its dependency on BE functions is minimal and solved by including `class.t3lib_befunc.php` in the FE plugin.

When the reference index is used, the system will show a number of references to the current record in the **List** module, and a clean-up script will be able to detect hanging files and remove them.

We are interested in the following function:

- `function updateRefIndexTable($table,$uid,$testOnly=FALSE)`

This function will examine the record and update the reference index. Here are some code examples:

```
require_once(PATH_t3lib . 'class.t3lib_befunc.php');
require_once(PATH_t3lib . 'class.t3lib_refindex.php');

$fields = array(
    // Fill array with fields
);
$GLOBALS['TYPO3_DB']->exec_INSERTquery('tx_myext_table',
    $fields);
$uid = $GLOBALS['TYPO3_DB']->sql_insert_id();
$refIndex = t3lib_div::makeInstance('t3lib_refindex');
/* @var $refIndex t3lib_refindex */
$refIndex->updateRefIndexTable('tx_myext_table', $uid);
```

This is all that has to be done to update the reference index. The `@var` comment helps modern PHP IDEs show code assist for the variable.

Hooks

Hooks in TYPO3 are special functions that the system calls while it performs some actions. Using hooks, extensions can modify a process in the middle, observe system state, pre- and post-process data, and do many other things.

Typically, a hook function is defined either as a regular function with `user_` prefix or as a class prefixed with `tx_extkey_`. Hooks are registered in the extension's `ext_localconf.php` file (see Chapter 2) in the following way:

```
$GLOBALS['TYPO3_CONF_VARS']['SC_OPTIONS']
    ['cms/layout/class.tx_cms_layout.php']
    ['list_type_Info']['extkey_pi1'][] =
    'EXT:extkey/class.tx_extkey_cms_layout.php
    :tx_extkey_cms_layout->getExtensionSummary';
```

This particular hook will provide additional information to the page module to display near the extension's instance.

Backend API

This part of the API is used in the Backend. It is not well known to developers because TYPO3 lacks documentation about this part of the API. We will cover the major parts of the Backend API code in this section.

TCEforms

TCEforms is visually familiar to anyone who has used TYPO3.

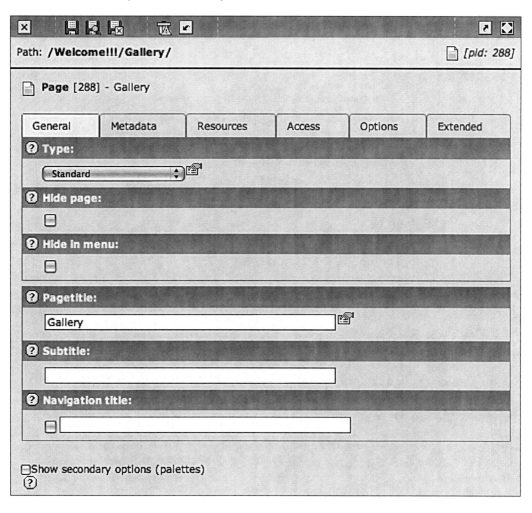

From a developer's viewpoint, TCEforms is an automated way of presenting the content of a database table to the user in a form suitable for editing. TCEforms reads the table configuration array (or TCA) for the table and builds controls dynamically according to the information in the TCA. The TCA for each TYPO3 core table is stored in the TYPO3 core. Extensions provide additional TCA entries for each extension table. If a TCA entry is not provided for the table, the TYPO3 Install tool will complain about it.

TCEforms is the most complex TYPO3 class you can use from. Its API was never meant for external use, but it is still possible to do it. Though this will not be described in this book, developers can figure it out by looking at the file `typo3/mod/user/ws/workspaceforms.php`. This file makes use of TCEforms to create custom rendering of workspace records.

TCEmain

TCEmain is the TYPO3 record processor. It handles the following tasks:

- Record creation, deletion, updation, copying, and moving
- Clearing the cache
- Version creation, updating, and publishing

Though this list does not contain all the functions, the class contains over 100 functions and nearly 5500 lines of code. The class name for TCEmain is `t3lib_TCEmain`.

Most extension developers are interested in the first two entries from the list above. We will review these in the later sections.

Record Manipulation

Record manipulation happens through two functions:

- `process_datamap()`
- `process_cmdmap()`

These functions do not take any parameters. Parameters must be passed to TCEmain's `start()` function. If both functions need to be executed, then `process_datamap()` should be called first.

The `process_datamap()` function takes care of record creation and updates. The `process_cmdmap()` function moves, deletes, undeletes, localizes, and creates versions for records.

Both functions expect their data to be in a certain format. As often in TYPO3, data consists of arrays.

The `process_cmdmap()` function uses the following format for data:

```
$datamap = array(
    $tableName => array(
        $recordUid => array(
            $fieldName => $fieldValue
        )
    )
);
```

Here, `$tableName` is the database table name. There can be any number of tables in the `$datamap`. The `$recordUid` variable is the unique identifier of the record (`uid` field in the database table). If `$recordUid` is a string and starts from NEW (followed by a random string), then a new record will be created in the database. `$fieldName` is a database field name (`uid` cannot be passed as a field). The `$fieldValue` variable is an unescaped (raw) field value. The `process_cmdmap()` function has additional useful features. For example, it is possible to create a page and its content elements at once. The `$recordUid` variable for the `pages` table will start with NEW, and `pid` field for each content element should have the same identifier. TCEmain will substitute `pid` values automatically. But do not try it with other fields, it will not work as it does with `pid`. You can also insert a record before another record. In this case, `pid` field should be a negative value of the other record's `uid` attribute.

After a record is created, it is possible to obtain record `uid` values from TCEmain. TCEmain's `substNEWwithIDs` attribute is an array where keys are NEW-style identifiers, and values are `uid` values for new database records.

The `process_cmdmap()` function has similar data format:

```
$cmdmap = array(
    $tableName => array(
        $recordUid => array(
            $command => $command_data
        )
    )
);
```

The next table shows values for `$command` and the format of `$command_data`.

Command	Command data format
Move	`uid` of the page where the record will be moved
copy	`uid` of the page where the record will be copied
localize	`uid` of the record from the `sys_language` table
version	Complex;.beyond the purpose of this book.
delete	empty
undelete	empty

The following code example will create a page with a single text element and delete this page with the element.

```
require_once(PATH_t3lib . 'class.t3lib_tcemain.php');
$pid = 'NEW' . uniqid('');
$content_uid = 'NEW' . uniqid('');
```

```
$tstamp = time();
// Datamap for page and content
$datamap = array(
    'pages' => array(
        $pid => array(
            'pid' => 1,
            'title' =>
                $GLOBALS['LANG']->getLL('my_page_title'),
            'hidden' => 0,
            // Next line says that page is "Standard"
            'doktype' => 1,
            'crdate' => $tstamp,
            'tstamp' => $tstamp,
            // Next line says what user created the page
            'cruser_id' => $GLOBALS['BE_USER']->user['uid'],
            // Set some permissions. See TSConfig document
            'perms_userid' =>
                $GLOBALS['BE_USER']->user['uid'],
            'perms_groupid' => 0, // No group
                'perms_user' => 31, // See TSConfig
                'perms_group' => 27,
                'perms_everyone' => 0,
        )
    ),
    'tt_content' => array(
        $content_uid => array(
            'pid' => $pid,
            'header' =>
                $GLOBALS['LANG']->getLL('content_title'),
                'CType' => 'text',
                'bodytext' => 'Hello, TYPO3!',
                'crdate' => $tstamp,
                'tstamp' => $tstamp,
                'cruser_id' =>
                    $GLOBALS['BE_USER']->user['uid'],
                'colPos' => 0
        )
    )
);
// Create TCEmain instance
$tce = t3lib_div::makeInstance('t3lib_TCEmain');
/* @var $tce t3lib_TCEmain */
$tce->start($datamap, null);
$tce->process_datamap();
```

```
if (count($tce->errorLog) != 0) {
    // $tce->errorLog is an array of error messages
}
// Prepare cmdmap to delete created records.
// BE user must have 'recursive delete' enabled
// for this example!
$cmdmap = array();
foreach ($tce->substNEWwithIDs as $new => $uid) {
    // $tce->substNEWwithIDs_table is like
    // $tce->substNEWwithIDs but contains
    // table names
    $cmdmap[$tce->substNEWwithIDs_table[$new]][$uid] =
    array('delete' => '');
}
$tce = t3lib_div::makeInstance('t3lib_TCEmain');
/* @var $tce t3lib_TCEmain */
$tce->start(null, $cmdmap);
$tce->process_cmdmap();
if (count($tce->errorLog) != 0) {
    // Process error messages
}
```

Clearing Cache

If an extension's work affects the content of the page in the FE, the extension must take care of clearing cache for the page. For example, if an extension generates new content, modifies existing content, or creates a record that should be displayed on the page, the page cache has to be cleared.

TCEmain is strictly BE code. But cache pages are written in the way that allows one to use them from FE as well.

There are several functions that can be used to clear cache. As extension developers, we are mostly interested in one. It is named clear_cacheCmd. This function accepts a single parameter. For our purpose, it should be page uid value.

A code example:

```
require_once(PATH_t3lib . 'class.t3lib_tcemain.php');
// Create TCEmain instance
$tce = t3lib_div::makeInstance('t3lib_TCEmain');
/* @var $tce t3lib_TCEmain */
$tce->clear_cacheCmd(123);
```

If more than one page has to be cleared, it has to be done in a loop.

Frontend API

This part of the API is used in the Frontend. The number of files is relatively small, but the number of functions is very large. We will review only major functions.

TSFE

TSFE (historically stands for "TypoScript Frontend") is the main FE class. It is sometimes called "page" object among developers. This class contains methods that determine page ID, parse TypoScript templates, execute templates, process output and cache it. Also, TSFE is responsible for managing FE user object. TSFE is located in the class `tslib_fe` (exercise: see if you can guess the path to the file name).

Normally, extensions do not call TSFE methods but use some TSFE class attributes. We will describe the most important attributes here:

- `additionalHeaderData`

    This is an array where FE plugins can add HTML tags that should appear between `<head>` and `</head>` on the page. It is a good practice to start with `tx_yourextkey_` prefix. Do not add inline `<script>` (`<script>` tag without `src` attribute) here!

- `additionalJavaScript`

    An array where FE plugins may add inline JavaScript, if necessary. It is a good practice to start with `tx_yourextkey_` prefix.

- `config`

    This is an array. It is the only member with the `config` key corresponding to the parsed `config` object from the current TypoScript setup. This array contains merged entries from `config` and `page.config`.

- `fe_user`

    An object of the class, `tslib_feUserAuth`, which represents a FE user. The `user` attribute of this class contains a record from the `fe_users` table. If FE user is logged in, `$GLOBALS['TSFE']->fe_user->user['uid']` will be set, and `t3lib_div::testInt` will return `true` for it.

- `id`

    This is the current page ID. It is very often used in FE plugins as `$GLOBALS['TSFE']->id`.

- `lang`

    This attribute is the current language code (string value). This is not the same as the ISO language code. It is TYPO3 code to be used with language files. The value `default` means English. A full list of codes can be found in `typo3/sysext/setup/mod/locallang.xml` as a set of `lang_*` entries.

- `page`

    This is a record from the `pages` table that corresponds to the current page. If the page is loaded in a nondefault language, this record will have that language applied (all fields like title or navigation title will be taken from `pages_language_overlay` and applied to this record).

- `pSetup`

    This is a parsed TypoScript setup for the plugin. This is useful in certain cases. For example, you may want to examine the setup of another plugin. It is a parsed TypoScript array.

- `register`

    This is an array of registers (see `LOAD_REGISTER` in TSRef). FE plugins can set registers, and they will be available to other objects on the page (plugins or TypoScript objects from TypoScript setup). The key is register name, value is register value.

- `rootLine`

    This is an array of records from the `pages` table that represents the path to the current page from the root of the website.

- `sys_language_content`

    This is a `uid` field value for the record in the `sys_language` table. TYPO3 will select content from the `tt_content` table with `sys_language_uid` that matches this value.

- `sys_language_uid`

    This is a `uid` field value for the record in the `sys_language` table. It corresponds to `config.sys_language_uid` in TypoScript setup.

- `sys_language_mode`
    See `config.sys_language_mode` in TSRef.

Content Objects

Content objects display information on the page. All content object types are described in TSRef and they are implemented by the class named `tslib_cObj`, which is located in `typo3/sysext/cms/tslib/class.tslib_content.php`. A quick look at this class reveals familiar names such as TEXT, HTML, USER, or stdWrap.

This class is used very often in FE plugins. It has lots of very well-documented methods. We will describe many of them in due course when we have to use them in our real extension.

Plugin API

Last but not the least in its importance is the `tslib_pibase` class. This is a base class for the FE plugins. While it is not mandatory to use it, most plugins do because this class provides many helpful methods. We will discuss this class in detail in Chapter 5 of the book. For now, we should know that this class provides the following function groups:

- Link generation
  These functions allow plugins to create links with plugin parameters in them.

- Handling of localized labels
  These functions help to retrieve translated labels from the language files.

- Frontend editing
  These functions help to add FE editing capabilities to plugins (rarely used by plugins).

- Database queries
  These functions do specialized database queries. Most of them are equivalents of the `t3lib_DB` functions.

- Flexform handling functions
  Flexform is a TYPO3 way of having forms inside forms. They are often used for plugin configuration. These functions initialize flexform data and extract information from flexforms.

Summary

In this chapter, we had a very brief overview of TYPO3 API. TYPO3 API is large, and it contains functions that cover almost every need of a typical extension developer. We will actively use TYPO3 API in our own extension in the forthcoming chapters of this book.

2
Anatomy of TYPO3 Extension

This chapter describes TYPO3 extensions from the developer's point of view. After reading this chapter, the reader will have basic knowledge of extension structure, files, and how extensions interact with TYPO3. This knowledge is necessary for extension planning and implementation.

TYPO3 Extension Categories

All TYPO3 extensions are classified into several predefined categories. These categories do not actually differentiate the extensions. They are more like hints for users about extension functionality. Often, it is difficult for the developer to decide which category an extension should belong to. The same extension can provide PHP code that fits into many categories. An extension can contain Frontend (FE) plugins, Backend (BE) modules, static data, and services, all at once. While it is not always the best solution to make such a monster extension, sometimes it is necessary. In this case, the extension author should choose the category that best fits the extension's purpose. For example, if an extension provides a reservation system for website visitors, it is probably FE related, even if it includes a BE module for viewing registrations. If an extension provides a service to log in users, it is most likely a service extension, even if it logs in FE users. It will be easier to decide where the extension fits after we review all the extension categories in this chapter.

Choosing a category for an extension is mandatory. While the TYPO3 Extension Manager can still display extensions without a proper category, this may change and such extensions may be removed from TER (TYPO3 Extension Repository) in the future.

The extension category is visible in several places. Firstly, extensions are sorted and grouped by category in the Extension Manager. Secondly, when an extension is clicked in the Extension Manager, its category is displayed in the extension details.

If an extension's category is changed from one to another, it does not affect extension functionality. The Extension Manager will show the extension in a different category. So, categories are truly just hints for the user. They do not have any significant meaning in TYPO3.

So, why do we care and talk about them? We do so because it is one of those things that make a good extension. If an extension developer starts making a new extension, they should do it properly from the very beginning. And one of the first things to do properly is to decide where an extension belongs.

So, let's look into the various extension categories in more detail.

Category: Frontend

Extensions that belong to the **Frontend** category provide functionality related to the FE. It does not mean that they generate website output. Typically, extensions from the FE category extend FE functionality in other ways. For example, they can transform links from standard `/index.php?id=12345` to `/news/new-typo3-book-is-out.htm`. Or, they can filter output and clean it up, compress, add or remove HTML comments, and so on. Often, these extensions use one or more hooks (see Chapter 1) in the FE classes. For example, TSFE (see Chapter 1) has hooks to process submitted data, or to post-filter content (and many others).

Examples of FE extensions are `source_optimization` and `realurl`.

Category: Frontend plugins

Frontend plugins is possibly the most popular extension category. Extensions from this category typically generate content for the website. They provide new content objects, or extend existing types of content objects (see Chapter 1).

Typical examples of extensions from the **Frontend plugins** category are `tt_news`, `comments`, `ratings`, etc.

Category: Backend

Extensions from the **Backend category** provide additional functionality for TYPO3 Backend. Often, they are not seen inside TYPO3 BE, but they still do some work. Examples of such extensions are various debugging extensions (such as `rlmp_filedevlog`) and extensions that add or change the pop-up menu in the BE (such as `extra_page_cm_options` system extension). This category is rarely used because extensions belonging to it are very special.

Category: Backend module

Extensions from this category provide additional modules for TYPO3 BE. Typical examples are system extensions such as `beuser` (provides **Tools** | **Users** module) or `tstemplate` (provides **Web** | **Template** module).

Category: Services

Services extend core TYPO3 functionality. Most known and most popular service extensions are authentication services. TYPO3 Extension Repository contains extensions to authenticate TYPO3 users over phpBB, vBulletine, or LDAP user databases.

Services are somewhat special and will not be covered in this book. Extension developers who are interested in the development of services should consult appropriate documentation on the `typo3.org` website.

Category: Examples

Extensions from this category provide examples. There are not many, and are typically meant for beginners or for those who want to learn a specific feature of TYPO3, or features that another TYPO3 extension provides.

Category: Templates

Extensions from this category provide templates. Most often, they have preformatted HTML and CSS files in order to use them with the `templateautoparser` extension or map with **TemplaVoila**. Sometimes, they also contain TypoScript templates, for example, `tmpl_andreas01` and `tmpl_andreas09` extensions. Once installed, they provide pre-mapped TemplaVoila templates for any website, making it easy to have a website up and running within minutes.

Category: Documentation

Documentation extensions provide TYPO3 documentation. Normally, TYPO3 extensions contain documentation within themselves, though sometimes, a document is too big to be shipped with extensions. In such cases, it is stored separately. There is an unofficial convention to start an extension key for such extensions with the `doc_` prefix (that is, `doc_indexed_search`).

Category: Miscellaneous

Everything else that does not fit into any other category goes here; typical examples are **skins**. But do not put your extension here if you just cannot decide where it fits. In all probability, it should go into one of the other categories, not into **Miscellaneous**.

Extension Files

TYPO3 extensions consist of several files. Some of these files have predefined names, and serve a predefined purpose. Others provide code or data but also follow certain naming conventions. We will review all the predefined files in this chapter and see what purpose they serve. We will look into the files according to their logical grouping.

While reading this section, you can take any extension from the `typo3conf/ext/` directory at your TYPO3 installation and check the contents of each discussed file. Some files may be missing if the extension does not use them. There is only one file which is mandatory for any TYPO3 extension, `ext_emconf.php`. We will start examining files starting from this one.

Common Files

All files from this group have predefined names, and TYPO3 expects to find certain information in them. Hacking these files to serve another purpose or to have a different format usually results in incompatibility with other extensions or TYPO3 itself. While it may work in one installation, it may fail in others. So, avoid doing anything non-standard with these files.

ext_emconf.php

This is the only required file for any TYPO3 extension. And this is the only file that should be modified with great care. If it is corrupt, TYPO3 will not load any extension.

This file contains information on the TYPO3 Extension Manager. This information tells the Extension Manager what the extension does, provides, requires, and conflicts with. It also contains a checksum for each file in the extension. This checksum is updated automatically when the extension is sent to TER (TYPO3 Extension Repository). The server administrator can easily check if anyone has hijacked the extension files by looking into the extension details in the Extension Manager. The modified files are shown in red. Here is a tip. If you (as an extension developer) send your own extension directly to the customer (bypassing TER upload), or plan to use it on your own server, always update the `ext_emconf.php` file using the `Backup/Delete` function of the Extension Manager. This will ensure that TYPO3 shows up-to-date data in the Extension Manager.

Here is an example of a `ext_emconf.php` file from the `smoothuploader` extension:

```php
<?php
############################################################
# Extension Manager/Repository config file for ext: ⏎
# "smoothuploader"
# Auto generated 29-02-2008 12:36
# Manual updates:
# Only the data in the array - anything else is removed by ⏎
# next write.
# "version" and "dependencies" must not be touched!
############################################################
$EM_CONF[$_EXTKEY] = array(
    'title' => 'SmoothGallery Uploader',
    'description' => 'Uploads images to SmoothGallery',
    'category' => 'plugin',
    'author' => 'Dmitry Dulepov [Netcreators]',
    'author_email' => 'dmitry@typo3.org',
    'shy' => '',
    'dependencies' => 'rgsmoothgallery',
    'conflicts' => '',
    'priority' => '',
    'module' => '',
    'state' => 'beta',
    'internal' => '',
    'uploadfolder' => 0,
    'createDirs' => '',
    'modify_tables' => 'tx_rgsmoothgallery_image',
    'clearCacheOnLoad' => 0,
    'lockType' => '',
    'author_company' => 'Netcreators BV',
    'version' => '0.3.0',
    'constraints' => array(
        'depends' => array(
            'rgsmoothgallery' => '1.1.1-',
        ),
        'conflicts' => array(
        ),
        'suggests' => array(
        ),
    ),
```

```
        '_md5_values_when_last_written' => 'a:12:{s:9:...;}',
        'suggests' => array(
        ),
    );
    ?>
```

The variable _md5_values_when_last_written is shortened in the listing above.

The following fields are used in the $EM_CONF array:

Field name	Field description
title	Extension title. This is visible in the Extension Manager and TYPO3 Extension Repository.
description	Description of the extension.
category	Category to which the extension belongs (discussed earlier in this chapter).
author	Extension author's name.
author_email	Extension author's e-mail.
author_company	Extension author's company.
shy	If set to **1**, the extension will be hidden if **Display shy extensions** is not checked in the Extension Manager. There are no valid reasons to make extensions shy. This flag is usually set for system extensions that appear in every TYPO3 installation. It just makes the Extension Manager less crowded.
dependencies	Obsolete; should not be used.
conflicts	Obsolete; should not be used.
priority	This field is used for prioritizing extensions in certain cases. Leave it untouched.
module	Lists extension's Backend modules. Left menu uses this field to find information about modules.
state	Can be one of the following values: • alpha Initial development, not ready for release, some functions may work, has bugs. • beta Ready for testing, may have bugs.

Field name	Field description
	• `stable` Extension is mature, can be used in production. • `experimental` Extension may change TYPO3 behavior in an unusual way or may do something unusual. It is important to change `state` appropriately during extension development. It is very common to see **beta** extensions that are used for years on many production sites. Unfortunately, this is typical in the open source software world; products stay beta for ages and never become **ready**. Do not follow this practice; set your extension's state to `stable` after you fix major bugs, and get positive feedback from users. **stable** does not mean you have to stop developing it. It means that other people may use it in production.
`internal`	Set if this extension is internal for TYPO3. May not be used by any custom extension.
`uploadfolder`	Obsolete, but still used. This declares the name of the directory, related to TYPO3 web root, where files will be uploaded. Currently, this serves only informational purposes because actual upload directories are declared for each database table in the table configuration array (`$TCA`). We will talk about it when we discuss `ext_tables.php` and `tca.php`.
`createDirs`	Comma delimited list of directories to be created during extension installation. Directories must be relative to TYPO3 web root directory.
`modify_tables`	Comma delimited list of tables modified by this extension. System tables or tables from other extensions can be modified by placing certain SQL into the `ext_tables.sql` file. Each table name follows certain naming conventions. If an extension modifies a table with a non matching name but does not list it in this property, the Extension Manager will show naming errors.
`clearCacheOnLoad`	If set, clears cache when the extension is installed. Useful only for extensions that modify website output immediately after installation (such as HTML clean-up extensions or content compressors). Do not set if not necessary.
`lockType`	This field allows to "lock" extensions to a certain type of installation (global, local, or system). Generally, this field should never be modified. Modification may cause problems with the installation of the extension.

Field name	Field description
version	This indicates the extension version. Normally modified by the Extension Manager when the extension is uploaded to TER. However, if the extension is private, the version should be modified manually each time the extension leaves the developer's computer. Version follows the PHP versioning pattern. It consists of three digits, each representing a change in one of the following things: • major version (also called release version) • minor version • bug fix version The first number is updated when the extension has a major change in behavior, such as major feature added, completely rewritten code, and so on. The second number is updated when the extension is developed, or some minor features are introduced. The last number is updated when the new version only fixes bugs.
constraints	This element consists of three sub-elements, all having an identical structure. Each sub-element is an array, where the array key is an extension key, and its value is zero, one, or two version numbers. A zero version number means that the constraint applies to any version of the extension while one and two numbers mean that the constraint applies to a version range. Two version numbers separated by a dash imply "from version – to version" (inclusive) and for one number, the versions of the extension to which the constraint applies depend on the position of the version number and the dash. Examples: • `'extkey' => ''` Applies to any version of the extension with an extension key extkey • `'extkey' => '1.0.0-'` Means that the constraint applies to the extension with version number 1.0.0 and higher • `'extKey' => '-1.0.0'` Means that all versions prior and including 1.0.0 are caught by this constraint • `'extkey' => '0.5.0-1.0.0'` Means that the constraint works for versions from 0.5.0 to 1.0.0 (both inclusive)

Field name	Field description
	There are three types of constraints:
	• `depends`
	The Extension Manager will require listed extensions to be installed before the current extension can be installed. Generally, it means that the current extension uses listed extensions in some way.
	• `conflicts`
	The Extension Manager will not allow installation of this extension if it is installed from this constraint. A version check in this constraint works in TYPO3 version 4.1.7 and higher.
	• `suggests`
	The Extension Manager will prompt for the installation of the extensions listed in this constraint, but will not insist on doing so. This constraint is useful when an extension extends many extensions all at once. For example, the `comments_ic` extension extends `tt_news` and `commerce` with an ability to close comments individually for each item. It suggests these two extensions for installation. Notice that it gives an error if these two extensions are placed into the `depends` constraint because then `comments_ic` may not be used only with `tt_news` (the Extension Manager will require `commerce` as well!)
`suggests`	Obsolete; do not use.

ext_conf_template.txt

This file contains the definitions of installation-wide system settings for the extension. Each setting is a name/value combination. Names and values are separated by an "equal to" sign. The spaces in name and value are stripped. Here is how such a configuration looks in the Extension Manager:

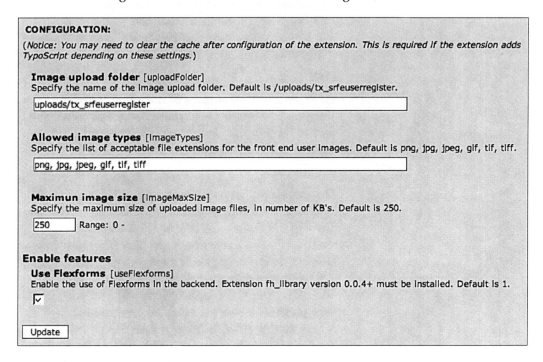

Each name/value pair can be prepended with a special comment. A comment defines data type, title, and description for each name/value pair. Here is an example:

```
# cat=basic/enable; type=string; label=Database  URLconnection string:
mnoGoSearch connection URL
dbaddr =  mysql://user:pass@host/dbname?dbmode=blob&LiveUpdates=yes
```

The first line is a special comment. It also consists of name/value pairs, separated by a semicolon. The value from this file serves as a default value.

The same syntax is used for TypoScript constants.

Name	Value
cat	Format is "category/subcategory: title" (title is usually omitted). This field is used to group settings. It is possible to have, for example, **database settings** separate from **rendering settings**. Valid values for categories are:

- basic
  Any general options, most likely to be changed. Mandatory database configuration is an example.

- menu
  Configuration for menu. This is rarely used for extension installation, but sometimes used for TypoScript constants.

- page
  Page-related options. Also, typically used for constants, not for extension installation.

- advanced
  Advanced options go here.

Categories may have subcategories. Available subcategories are:

- enable
  Used for options that enable or disable primary functions of a template.

- dims
  Dimensions of all kinds; pixels, widths, heights of images, frames, cells, and so on.

- file
  Files such as background images, fonts, and so on.

- typo
  Typography and related constants (rarely used).

- color
  Color setup (rarely used).

- links
  Usually used for link targets.

- language
  Language related settings.

Name	Value
type	A field will be rendered according to its type. Valid field types are:

- `string`
  This is a default type. It is just a string with no conversion or validation.
- `int`
  Integer number (or 0 if a noninteger is entered).
- `int+`
  Positive integer number (or 0 if a noninteger is entered).
- `color`
  HTML color (with color selector control).
- `file[extension-list]`
  File selector, will allow selection of only the files with extensions from the list.
- `wrap`
  HTML to wrap around content.
- `boolean`
  Rendered as a checkbox, and has two state values.
- `options[option-list]`
  A comma-delimited list (without spaces!) as label/value pairs.

Name	Value
label	Label and description, separated by a colon

These settings are saved by the Extension Manager and can be accessed programmatically:

```
$sysconf = unserialize($GLOBALS['TYPO3_CONF_VARS']['EXT']
                ['extConf']['extkey']);
if ($sysconf['enable']) {
```

These settings are used when they are system-wide. Anything which is site-dependent should go into the TypoScript setup for FE plugins (see the following section).

ext_tables.php

This file performs three functions:

- Declares extension tables.
- Declares fields for system or other extension tables extended by this extension.
- FE plugins and BE modules are registered with TYPO3 in this file.

The table definitions look quite simple. This information adds the definition of a new table to the TYPO3 global variable named $TCA (TCA stands for "Table Configuration Array").

The variable $TCA is one of the most important variables in TYPO3. It is an array where keys are database table names, and values are arrays of certain structure that define how fields in the database should look in TYPO3 BE forms, and also which fields have special meaning.

Each table definition in $TCA consists of several sections but ext_tables.php declares only one section, named ctrl. This saves a lot of memory if the table is not being used in a particular execution because table definitions may be really huge. TYPO3 includes all ext_tables.php files from all extensions. Thus, all tables are known to TYPO3. If necessary, TYPO3 will load a full table definition using the dynamicConfigFile property from the ctrl section.

Additionally, the ctrl section contains other important fields such as table name, table icon, and a list of fields that serve a special purpose.

Here is an example of a table definition from ext_tables.php:

```php
$TCA['tx_ratings_iplog'] = array(
    'ctrl' => array (
        'title'    =>   'LLL:EXT:ratings/locallang_db.xml:tx_ratings_
iplog',
        'label'    => 'reference',
        'tstamp'   => 'tstamp',
        'crdate'   => 'crdate',
        'cruser_id' => 'cruser_id',
        'default_sortby' => 'ORDER BY crdate DESC',
        'dynamicConfigFile' =>   t3lib_extMgm::extPath($_EXTKEY).'tca.
php',
        'iconfile'  => t3lib_extMgm::extRelPath($_EXTKEY) .
                'icon_tx_ratings_iplog.gif',
    ),
);
```

Information on ctrl and other sections can be found in the **TYPO3 Core API** document on the typo3.org website.

Tables are extended in a similar way. But instead of defining the `ctrl` section, new columns are defined and added to the existing tables using TYPO3 functions. We will talk more about column definition syntax in the section about `tca.php`. Here we will just see one example:

```
// New columns
$tempColumns = array(
    'tx_ratings_enable' => array(
        'exclude' => 1,
        'label' =>  'LLL:EXT:ratings/locallang_db.xml:tt_news.tx_
ratings_enable',
        'config' => array(
            'type'      => 'check',
            'items'     => array(
                array('', '')
            ),
            'default'   => '1'
        )
    ),
);
t3lib_div::loadTCA('tt_news');
t3lib_extMgm::addTCAcolumns('tt_news', $tempColumns, 1);
t3lib_extMgm::addToAllTCAtypes('tt_news', ↵ 'tx_ratings_
enable;;;;1-1-1');
```

Here, one new column is defined for the `tt_news` table. The definition is set to `$tempColumns`. The column is set to type `check`, which means that an additional checkbox will be displayed in the `tt_news` item. All configuration options for `check` and other column types are explained in the **TYPO3 Core API** document.

The last three lines add the above definition to the TCA. The first line loads the full TCA definition for the `tt_news` table. This is necessary because the `ext_tables.php` file includes only the `ctrl` section for each table. The next line actually adds a new column definition to the table. The third line tells TYPO3 where to display this new column. In this particular case, it just added the new column to the end of the existing fields. It is possible to put columns before or after the existing fields too. See the documentation for `t3lib_extMgm::addToAllTCAtypes` in the source code for more information.

The FE plugin addition looks like this:

```
t3lib_extMgm::addPlugin(array(
 'LLL:EXT:ratings/locallang_db.xml:tt_content.list_type_pi1',
 $_EXTKEY . '_pi1'), 'list_type');
```

Usually, this code is generated automatically when a new extension is created. The first parameter is an array. It associates the plugin with a human-readable name of the plugin. The second parameter tells TYPO3 about the type of the plugin. Normally, it is `list_type` but it can also have another value (for example, site maps).

ext_tables.sql

This file includes database table definitions written in SQL. TYPO3 extensions may define their own tables or extend existing system or other extension tables. These two cases are different and require different SQL statements.

If an extension defines its own tables, syntax of such a definition should exactly be the same as produced by the SHOW CREATE TABLE SQL statement in the MySQL console. (Even if the actual database is Oracle or MSSQL, definitions must have MySQL syntax). No additional spaces (or missing spaces) and no position change for field modifiers is allowed. This limitation exists due to the fact that TYPO3 parses SQL to see if it needs to update the table structure. The only parts that can be removed are the CHARACTER SET, ENGINE, and COLLATE directives. The following example shows a table definition from the `ratings` extension. It has ENGINE set to InnoDB to ensure high concurrency of data.

```
#
# Table structure for table 'tx_ratings_data'
#
CREATE TABLE tx_ratings_data (
    uid int(11) NOT NULL auto_increment,
    pid int(11) DEFAULT '0' NOT NULL,
    tstamp int(11) DEFAULT '0' NOT NULL,
    crdate int(11) DEFAULT '0' NOT NULL,
    cruser_id int(11) DEFAULT '0' NOT NULL,
    reference text NOT NULL,
    rating int(11) DEFAULT '0' NOT NULL,
    vote_count int(11) DEFAULT '0' NOT NULL,
    PRIMARY KEY (uid),
    KEY parent (pid),
    KEY reference (reference(16))
) ENGINE = InnoDB;
```

Another case is table modification. Normally, such changes are made with ALTER TABLE SQL statements, but TYPO3 uses another way, partial table definitions. Here is an example from the same `ratings` extension:

```
#
# Table structure for table 'tt_news'
#
CREATE TABLE tt_news (
    tx_ratings_enable int(1) DEFAULT '1' NOT NULL,
);
```

It looks like a normal CREATE TABLE statement except that it does not have all the fields required by TYPO3 (such as uid and pid) and has a comma after the definition of the tx_ratings_enable field. So technically, such SQL is neither valid nor does it represent a valid TYPO3 table. But it tells TYPO3 that the Extension Manager should merge the tt_news table definition from some other extension with this definition and update the table to show the result of the merge, if necessary.

No other SQL statements can appear in this file.

ext_tables_static+adt.sql

This file is very similar to ext_tables.sql except that it has table creation statements for static tables and may have data definition statements (SQL INSERT statements).

Static tables contain information that does not change. For example, the static_info_tables extension contains static tables with language codes, taxes, currencies, country names, character sets, and so on. This information never changes while TYPO3 is running (though it may be updated if the tax rate changes). So, it is inserted statically.

The table definition statements do not differ from those in ext_tables.sql.

The data definition statements are simple SQL INSERT statements. They must insert all fields (including automatically incrementing uid field), and must not use MySQL extended INSERT syntax. The easiest way to create proper statements is to add data to the database manually and use the mysqldump program with c -n -d -compact -extended-insert=FALSE options to export data.

ext_localconf.php

This file usually contains hook definitions and registers TypoScript from the FE plugins with TYPO3. Here is an example from the irfaq extension:

```
// Add plugin's TypoScript
t3lib_extMgm::addPItoST43($_EXTKEY,  'pi1/class.tx_irfaq_pi1.php',
'_pi1', 'list_type', 1);
// TCEmain hooks for managing related entries
$GLOBALS ['TYPO3_CONF_VARS'] ['SC_OPTIONS']
   ['t3lib/class.t3lib_tcemain.php']
   ['processDatamapClass'] ['irfaq'] =
      'EXT:irfaq/class.tx_irfaq_tcemain.php:tx_irfaq_tcemain';
$GLOBALS ['TYPO3_CONF_VARS'] ['SC_OPTIONS']
   ['t3lib/class.t3lib_tcemain.php']
   ['processCmdmapClass'] ['irfaq'] =
   'EXT:irfaq/class.tx_irfaq_tcemain.php:tx_irfaq_tcemain';
```

Notice how TYPO3 file references are used in hook declaration.

ext_icon.gif

This is an icon to show in the Extension Manager, to the left of extension title. An icon should be a 16x16 pixels, nonanimated, transparent GIF. Many extensions use 18x16 pixels because it looks better in the Extension Manager. But the TYPO3 Extension Repository expects a 16x16 pixels image and will stretch it to this size.

tca.php

This file contains complete TCA definitions for each table. It is included when code calls the `t3lib_div::loadTCA` function with a table name. TYPO3 then looks in the `ctrl` section in `$TCA` for this table. It locates the `dynamicConfigFile` property and loads the corresponding file.

Let's see what this file looks like. We will look at the `ratings` extension again. The following example is long and it shows three columns with their definitions.

```
$TCA['tx_ratings_data'] = array(
    'ctrl' => $TCA['tx_ratings_data']['ctrl'],
    'columns' => array (
        'reference' => array(
        'exclude' => 1,
            'label' =>  'LLL:EXT:ratings/locallang_db.xml:tx_ratings_
data.reference',
            'config' => array(
                'type' => 'group',
                'internal_type' => 'db',
                'allowed' => '*',
                'size' => 1,
                'minitems' => 1,
                'maxitems' => 1,
            )
        ),
        'rating' => array(
            'exclude' => 1,
            'label' =>  'LLL:EXT:ratings/locallang_db.xml:tx_ratings_
data.rating',
            'config' => array(
                'type'      => 'input',
                'size'      => '4',
                'max'       => '4',
                'eval'      => 'int',
                'checkbox' => '0',
                'range'     => array(
                'upper' => '1000',
                    'lower' => '10'
```

```
                    ),
                    'default' => 0
                )
            ),
            'vote_count' => array(
                'exclude' => 1,
                'label' =>  'LLL:EXT:ratings/locallang_db.xml:tx_ratings_
    data.vote_count',
                'config' => array (
                    'type'     => 'input',
                    'size'     => '4',
                    'max'      => '4',
                    'eval'     => 'int',
                    'checkbox' => '0',
                    'range'    => array (
                    'upper' => '1000',
                    'lower' => '10'
                    ),
                    'default' => 0
                )
            ),
        ),
        'types' => array(
            '0' => array(
                'showitem' => 'reference;;;;1-1-1,
                            rating, vote_count')
        ),
    );
```

First, the original `ctrl` section is set to `$TCA`. There is no need to duplicate it from `ext_tables.php`. It is easier to set it to the existing value. Next is the `columns` section. It contains definitions for each column. Definitions are explained in the **TYPO3 Core API** document, and the reader is encouraged to look up what each definition in the example means. Notice that each field type has its own set of properties. For example, `input` type has an `eval` property, which may trim the field value or convert it to a date. This property does not exist for other field types. Always look for properties in the **TYPO3 Core API** document. Specifying a property with a hope that it will work is useless if the property is not defined in the **TYPO3 Core API** document.

One important feature of TCA is its record types. One field in the table can be designated as a `type` field. When the `type` field changes, the BE form for the record is reloaded, and another set of fields is shown. Type fields are defined in the `ctrl` section using the `type` property. The value of the `type` field (usually integer) is mapped to keys in the `types` section of the table definition in TCA (see previous example). If there is no `type` field for the table, the default value 0 is used as type.

The `types` section in the TCA definition for the table shows which fields are available in the form, and in which order. Again, "TYPO3 Core API" describes how this section looks. In the simplest case, it just lists fields. It is very important to remember that a field will not be shown in the form if it is not included in the `types` definition.

Another interesting feature of TCA is the display of conditions and the `requestUpdate` fields.

As we saw earlier, the `type` field can change the look of the form. But sometimes it is not enough, and some fields can be shown or hidden depending on the value of the other fields. The `displayCond` property exists, and the field can be shown or hidden depending on the condition. Conditions may be set depending on the other fields in the same record, extension status (installed or not), record status (new or not). Newer TYPO3 versions may introduce other conditions.

The `requestUpdate` fields are similar to the `type` field because they cause the form to reload when the value of the field changes. They do not have anything similar to the `types` section in TCA, but conditions may use the value of these fields to show or hide other fields. This allows us to create truly dynamic and rich forms. There is only one thing to bear in mind: do not become obsessed with the technical possibilities and forget to think about the user who is going to work with forms! All these technical possibilities are made for better user satisfaction, but they must be used with care. It is easy to create a form that will change too often and irritate users. So, just be careful!

class.ext_update.php

If this file is present in the extension, the Extension Manager will add a new function to the list of functions available for the extension. The function is named UPDATE!. When a user chooses the function, the Extension Manager will load the file and pass control to the class. The class can propose updates to the user and perform these updates when the user confirms them. For example, this class may convert the extension's database structure from old to new, or change values of fields using complex logic. This file is so rarely used that most extension developers are completely unaware of this feature.

The class in this file must be named ext_update. It must include at least the following two public methods:

- access

  The Extension Manager calls this method when a user clicks on the extension title in the Extension Manager and asks for details. If the method returns true, the Extension Manager will add an additional item to the list of functions. The item will be named "UPDATE!".

  This method is typically used to check if an update should be performed at all. The method name is historical but misleading because the Extension Manager is visible only to "admin" users, and admin users always have access to everything.

- main

  This method generates content. Typically, it is a list of things to update and an HTML form with a button to confirm these updates. When a user clicks the button, ext_update performs the necessary updates.

Frontend Plugin Files

FE plugins generate custom content for websites. Typical examples of FE plugins are photo galleries, guestbooks, news systems, and reports.

FE plugins in TYPO3 do not have many requirements from the TYPO3 side. Plugins must follow TYPO3 naming conventions (see Chapter 1 of this book) and must return content instead of outputting it directly. The simplest FE plugin file will contain a function, whose name starts with user_. The function will accept two arguments and will return a string (generated HTML content). While it is possible to make plugins this way, plugins are typically made as classes that extend a special system class (tslib_pibase). The tslib_pibase class provides many convenient methods for FE plugins such as localization handling, parameter gathering, and link generation.

pi Files

Typically, FE plugins are located in subdirectories prefixed by `pi` and followed by a number inside the extension (for example, `pi1`, `pi2`, etc). The numbers are not significant and do not have to be consecutive. However, plugin class name typically reflects the directory in its name (for example, `pi1/class.tx_extkey_pi1.php`).

There can be other files in the `pi` directory. There can be additional class files, which must follow naming conventions as usual (for example, class `tx_myext_myclass` in `class.tx_myext_myclass.php`). External files can be included in the `lib/` subdirectory (unofficial convention). Templates are typically included in the `res/` subdirectory inside the `pi` directory, which is in the extension's directory.

TypoScript Templates

Often, FE plugins require certain TypoScript to be set. Such TypoScript may include references to templates or page IDs where records are stored. The TypoScript files are named `constants.txt` and `setup.txt`, and can be located either in the extension's directory, or in another subdirectory. If one of the files is empty, it is usually omitted. This saves some parsing time for TYPO3.

Files from the extension's directory are loaded by TYPO3 automatically and made available automatically everywhere in the FE. However, this slows down the FE and currently it is recommended that you put TypoScript files into a separate directory and include them manually in the main TypoScript setup of the website through the `Web>Template` module. Administrators will choose to edit the whole template record in that module and use **Include static (from extensions)** to include the extension's template in the main template.

To register an extension's TypoScript templates with TYPO3, the following code is included into the extension's `ext_tables.php` file:

```
t3lib_extMgm::addStaticFile($_EXTKEY, 'static/Ratings/',
    'Ratings');
```

Here, the first parameter uses the variable that TYPO3 has automatically set to the value of the extension key before the inclusion of `ext_tables.php`. The next parameter is the relative path to the directory where `constants.txt` and `setup.txt` are located. The last parameter is the title of the template as shown in "Include static (from extensions)". This title is usually not localized (and it is in English!) because it is normally referred to by this name in the extension's manual.

Backend Module and its Files

Backend modules are usually located in the subdirectories prefixed by `mod` and followed by a number. A Backend module's mandatory file is named `conf.php`. It contains a description of the module. Here is an example of such a file:

```php
<?php
    // DO NOT REMOVE OR CHANGE THESE 3 LINES:
define('TYPO3_MOD_PATH',
            '../typo3conf/ext/loginusertrack/mod1/');
$BACK_PATH = '../../../../typo3/';
$MCONF['name'] = 'web_txloginusertrackM1';

$MCONF['access'] = 'user,group';
$MCONF['script'] = 'index.php';
$MLANG['default']['tabs_images']['tab'] = 'moduleicon.gif';
$MLANG['default']['ll_ref'] =
            'LLL:EXT:loginusertrack/mod1/locallang_mod.php';
?>
```

First, three code lines define paths to the module. They are updated by the Extension Manager when the extension is installed. The next line defines who can access the module. It can have one of the following values:

- `user`
  Access can be granted to the BE users on an individual basis.

- `group`
  Access can be granted to the BE user groups.

- `user,group`
  Access can be granted to BE users and/or groups. This is a typical setting.

- `admin`
  This indicates that the module is available only for admin users.

There is one important constraint. If the module resides in another module (for example, in `User Tools` or `Admin Tools`), and the user has no access to the parent module, then the current module will be not be accessible either. For example, if the module is placed inside the `Tools` module, it does not make sense to make it accessible to BE users and/or groups by mentioning `user,group` in the `conf.php` file. This is because the `Tools` module is accessible only to admin users.

The module name declares where the module is located. The part before the underscore is the parent's module name. For a top-level module, there is no underscore in the module name. However, introducing new top level modules should be avoided.

The line with the `script` property in `$MCONF` defines a file to be called when this module is accessed through TYPO3 module menu. Typically, it is `index.php`, which sometimes allows calling the module directly from the browser's address bar.

The remaining two lines define the icon and label for the module in the left module menu.

The module script defines a class that follows naming conventions. Typically, it is `tx_extkey_module1`. The number in the end corresponds to the number of `mod` directories.

Module Function Files

Some modules allow you to add functions. An example of such a module is `Web>Functions` or `Web>Info`. Functions are selected in the top selector box of the module.

Additional module functions from extensions are placed in directories prefixed with `modfunc`, and followed by a number. The class name follows certain naming conventions. Typically, it is named `tx_extkey_modfunc1`, and is located in the file, `class.tx_extkey_modfunc1.php`. A class must have a method named `main` without parameters, which returns the module function's content.

Module functions are registered with modules using code that looks similar to this code:

```
if (TYPO3_MODE == 'BE') {
    t3lib_extMgm::insertModuleFunction(
        'tools_em',
        'tx_kickstarter_modfunc1',
        t3lib_extMgm::extPath($_EXTKEY) .
            'modfunc1/class.tx_kickstarter_modfunc1.php',
            'LLL:EXT:kickstarter/locallang_db.xml:
            moduleFunction.tx_kickstarter_modfunc1');
}
```

The first parameter of `t3lib_extMgm::insertModuleFunction` tells the module where to insert this new function. The next parameter is the function's class name. The third parameter is the function's file path, and the last parameter is the function's name from the module menu. All entries inside **Web | Info** are made from the additional functions shown in the following figure.

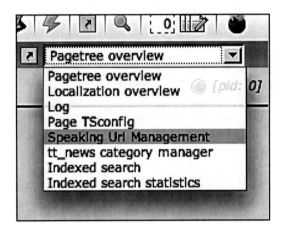

Documentation Files

Normally, there is a single documentation file in an extension. It is always named `manual.sxw` and located in the `doc/` subdirectory in the extension's directory.

Manuals must follow a certain format to be visible on the `typo3.org` website in the **Documentation** section. They must be OpenOffice 1.0 files, and must use the template available from the **Documentation** section of the `typo3.org` website under the title, **Documentation template**. There are instructions in this template about using styles and images. They must be followed for proper documentation.

Summary

In this section, we learned about extension files and extension classes. Now, the reader will have a basic knowledge of the extension structure and the extension components. In the forthcoming chapters, we will take a deeper look into extensions, and at coding our own extensions.

3
Planning Extensions

In this chapter, we will discuss why planning an extension is important, and how to plan an extension. Planning issues related to web development are covered in depth in many specialized books. Here, we will cover planning only with regard to TYPO3 extensions. By the end of the chapter, we will plan our own extension that we will develop until the end of this book.

Why is Planning Important?

Most open source developers see planning as a boring task. Why plan if one can just go and code? The answer is as simple as the question: The "Go and code" approach does not let us create truly optimal code. Portions of code have to be changed while other portions are written. They often lead to redundant code or uninitialized variables, partially covered conditions, and wrong return results. Code gets a "do not touch" reputation because changing anything renders the whole project unstable. Often the code works, but the project is more a failure than a success because it cannot be extended or re-used.

Another reason for planning is the ease of bug fixing and the costs associated with it. Open source developers often do not think about it until they start selling their services or work to commercial companies.

As shown by recent studies, the cost of problem fixing grows rapidly toward the end of the project. The cost is minimal when development has not started yet, and the person in charge just collects requirements. When requirements are collected and a programmer (or a team of programmers) starts to think how to implement these requirements, a change of requirements, or fixing a problem in the requirements still does not cost much. But it may already be difficult for developers if they came to a certain implementation approach after reviewing requirements. Things become worse at the development stage. Imagine that the selected approach was wrong and it was uncovered close to the end of development. Lots of time is lost, and work may have to start from the beginning. Now imagine what happens if the project is released to the customer and the customer says that the outcome of the project does not work as expected (something was implemented differently (as compared to expectations), or something was not implemented at all). The cost of fixing is likely to be high and overshoot the budget. Next, imagine what would happen if problems occurred when a project went live.

After reading the previous paragraph, some developers may ask how the situation applies to noncommercial development, as there is a false perception that there are no costs associated with it (at least, no direct costs). But, the costs exist! And often they are much more sensitive than financial costs. The cost in non-commercial development is reputation. If a developer's product does not work well or does not work at all or it has obvious flaws, the general opinion about the developer may become bad ("cannot trust his code"). Developers will also have troubles improving because often they do not understand what has gone wrong. But the answer is near. Do not rush! Plan it well! You may even think of something about the future code, and then start coding only when the picture is clear.

Planning is an important part of software development. While freelancers can usually divide their time freely between planning and implementation, many corporate developers often do not have such freedom. And even worse, many managers still do not see planning as a necessary step in software development. This situation is well explained in *The parable of the two programmers*, which readers of this book are encouraged to read in full.

When it comes to TYPO3, planning is more important than an average application. TYPO3 is very complex, and its implementation is also complex. Without planning, programmers will most likely have to change their already written code to fix unforeseen problems therefore, good planning for TYPO3 extensions is extremely important.

But let us move on and see how to plan an extension.

How to Plan

There are several stages in planning. Typically, each stage answers one or more important questions about development. TYPO3 developers should think about at least three stages:

- Gathering requirements
- Implementation planning
- Documentation planning

Of course, each project is unique and has other stages. But these three stages generally exist in every project.

Gathering Requirements

The first thing that a developer needs to know is what his/her extension will do. While it sounds pretty obvious, not many extension authors know exactly what functionality the extension has in the end. It evolves over time, and often the initial idea is completely different from the final implementation. Predictably, neither the original nor the final is done well.

In the other case, when extension features are collected, though planned and implemented according to plan, they usually fit well together.

So, the very first thing to do when creating an extension is to find out what that extension should do. This is called gathering requirements.

For noncommercial extensions, gathering requirements simply means writing down what each extension should do. For example, for a news extension, it may be:

- Show list of news sorted by date
- Show list of latest news
- Show news archive
- Show only a small amount of text in news list view

As we have seen, gathering requirements looks easier than it actually is. The process, however, may become more complex when an extension is developed for an external customer.

Alan Cooper, in his famous *About Face* book, shows how users, architects, and developers see the same product. From the user's perspective, it looks like a perfect circle. An architect sees something closer to an octagon. A developer creates something that looks like a polygon with many segments connected at different degrees. These differences always exist and each participating party is interested in minimizing them. A developer must not be afraid of asking questions. The cleaner picture he/she has, the better he will understand the customer's requirements.

Implementation Planning

When the requirements are gathered, it is necessary to think which blocks an extension will have. It may be blocks responsible for data fetching, presentation, conversion, and so on. In the case of TYPO3 extension implementation, planning should result in a list of Frondend (FE) plugins, Backend (BE) modules, and standalone classes. The purpose of each plugin, module, and/or class must be clear.

When thinking of FE plugins, caching issues must be taken into account. While most of the output can be cached to improve TYPO3 performance, forms processing should not be cached. Some extensions completely prevent caching of the page when processing forms. But there is a better approach, a separate FE plugin from the noncached output.

BE modules must take into account the ease of use. Standard BE navigation is not very flexible, and this must be taken into account when planning BE modules.

Certain functionalities can be moved to separate classes. This includes common functions, and any public APIs that an extension provides to the other extensions. Hooks or "user functions" are usually placed in separate classes depending on the functional zone or hooked class.

Documentation Planning

A good extension always comes with documentation. Documentation should also be planned. Typically, manuals for extensions are created using standard templates, which have standard sections defined. While this simplifies documentation writing for extension developers, they still have to plan what they will put into these sections.

TYPO3-Specific Planning

There are several planning issues specific to TYPO3. Developers must take care of them before the actual development.

Extension Keys

Each extension must have a unique key. Extension keys can be alphanumeric and contain underscore characters. It may not start with a digit, the letter u, or the `test_` prefix. However, not every combination of these symbols makes a good extension key.

An extension key must be descriptive but not too long. Having personal or company prefixes is not forbidden but is not recommended. Underscores should be avoided. Abbreviations should be avoided as well, because they often do not make sense for other users.

Examples of good extension keys are:

- news
- comments
- usertracker
- loginbox

Examples of bad extension keys are:

- news_extension
- mycorp_ustr
- myverygoodextensionthatdoesalotofthings
- mvgetdalot
- john_ext
- div2007

Database Structure

Most TYPO3 extensions use a database to load and/or store their own data. Changing the data structure during application development may seriously slow down development, or may even cause damage to data if some data is already entered into the system. Therefore, it is extremely important to think about an extension's data structure well in advance. Such thinking requires knowledge about how TYPO3 database tables are organized.

Tables in TYPO3 database must have certain structures to be properly managed by TYPO3. If a table does not fulfill TYPO3 requirements, users may see error messages in the BE (especially in **Web | List** module), and data may become corrupted.

Every record in every TYPO3 table belongs to a certain page inside TYPO3. TYPO3 has a way to identify which page the record belongs to.

Field Names

TYPO3 requires each table to have two fields with predefined names:

- uid
  This is a unique record identifier. It must be an auto incremented integer field.

- pid
  This field identifies which page the record belongs to. If this field is zero, it indicates that the page belongs to the "root level" (Globe icon in the TYPO3 page tree).

There are other fields (optional), whose names can be changed by configuration of the table. But typically, they are kept the same in every table:

- `crdate`
  Holds a record's creation date and time as Unix time stamp value.

- `tstamp`
  Holds a record's last modification date and time as Unix time stamp value.

- `deleted`
  If set to a nonzero value, the record is considered deleted (neither shown in the BE, nor available in the FE). Deleted records stay in the database and can be recovered by certain extensions. If this field is not defined, records are truly deleted from the database.

- `hidden`
  If set to a nonzero value, the record is hidden (not shown in the FE).

- `starttime`
  Date and time when a record becomes available (shown in the FE) as Unix time stamp.

- `endtime`
  Date and time when a record stops being available (shown in the FE) as Unix time stamp.

- `cruser_id`
  The `uid` value of the Backend user who created this record. Typically zero if the record is created by the FE plugin.

- `fe_group`
  An FE user can access the record only if the user belongs to one or more groups from this list. Meaning of "access" depends on the application, but usually it means that the record is completely inaccessible to users outside these groups.

- `l18n_parent`
  Related to localization of records.

- `l18n_diffsource`
  Related to localization of records.

- `sys_language_uid`
  Related to localization of records.

Several other fields are optional, but their names are reserved by TYPO3. They are related to workspace and version handling:

- t3ver_oid
- t3ver_id
- t3ver_wsid
- t3ver_label
- t3ver_state
- t3ver_stage
- t3ver_count
- t3ver_tstamp
- t3ver_move_id
- t3_origuid

Other field names are free to use.

Depending on the purpose of the field and its data type inside TYPO3, fields in the database table usually belong to one of the following types:

TYPO3 data type	Database type
Input field	varchar
	tinytext
	int
Text area (including RTE)	text
Check box	Int
Radio button	
Select box (simple values)	Int
Select box (database relation)	varchar
Database relation	varchar
	int (sometimes possible, but not recommended)
	text
Read-only	varchar
Custom field	int
	text

One question that extension developers often ask is why simple int fields are not recommended for database relations. The answer lies in the way TYPO3 stores references to records. Typically, it is the uid value of another record but it can also have a table name prepended (such as tt_content_10). TYPO3 understands both formats, and the second format makes it possible to use one field to relate to records in different tables. Obviously, the int field may not hold all this information.

When an extension is generated, a database table structure is generated along with other files. Therefore, if extension functions are planned properly, only minimal modifications may be needed during the development process.

Indexes

Indexes are the most successful but tricky aspects of databases. Database indexes help to select data faster. This topic is very large and we can discuss it only at a very basic level.

By default, TYPO3 generates two indexes: one for `uid` and another for `pid` columns. The first one selects a record by its unique identifier, while the second speeds up queries for the **Web | List** module.

Developers should add queries that help their extensions fetch data faster. Here are some tips for creating better indexes.

Many indexes on separate fields do not help. MySQL uses one index at a time. Therefore, if a query consists of many fields, one or more fields should be added to the index. However, if the index is too large, MySQL may choose to ignore it and scan the whole table for the records. Therefore, an index should not consist of more than three to four fields.

Fields in the index should be listed in the same order as they are listed in the query. This helps MySQL choose a proper index.

If a query uses sorting, the sorting field should be included as the last field of the index. If it is not at the end of the index, it is likely that MySQL will ignore the index.

Any `text` or `varchar` field should have length specification in the index to minimize the index length.

The `EXPLAIN` MySQL statement will help a developer identify how indexes are used. It should be used on a real set of data because it uses data to evaluate the query.

Database Relations

There are three types of database relations in TYPO3:

- Traditional relations
- Many-to-many relations (MM)
- Inline relational record editing (IRRE)

Traditional relations appeared first in TYPO3. They can hold one-way and (from one table to another only) two-way references. When traditional relations are used, relations to another table are stored in the referring table as a number (the `uid` of the record in another table) or as a table name with an underscore character and the `uid` value. The latter syntax allows reference to any record in the system.

Many-to-many (MM) relations use a separate table to store relations between two tables. Such relations are always two-way relations. A special field is still present in both of the referred tables, but it holds a number of relations for quick checking references. While this method is fully supported by TYPO3, it is rarely used. It requires additional queries and more work on maintaining references and ensuring that there are no dead ends. The other disadvantage of MM relations is that it is hard to understand references with only a quick glance at the data. It requires certain concentration on several database fields in MM tables, which makes it harder to debug problems with relations. But otherwise, MM relations are better than traditional relations. Computer science prefers this relation type to all the others.

Inline relational record editing (IRRE) appears last. It allows us to edit related records as a part of the main record. There are many ways to store data when IRRE is used. The whole IRRE subject is huge, complex and may not fit this book. We recommend anyone interested in IRRE to search for IRRE documentation on the `typo3.org` website.

When it comes to practice, extension developers usually use traditional relations. These relations are the fastest and easiest and are tested by years of successful work.

Planning Our Extension

In this section, we will plan the extension that we are going to create in this book. We will create a "FE user list and statistics" extension. Let's look at what this extension will do.

Requirements

Let's start by defining some requirements for our extension.

Functionality

The extension must perform the following tasks:

- Show a list of Frontend users in the Frontend
  - The list of fields must be customizable by the extension user with the following fields visible by default:

- User login name
- User real name
- Registration date
- Last visit
  - ○ Use pagination if the list is long
  - ○ Link record in the list to show single user information
- Show single user information with a customizable set of fields
- Show Frontend user list in the Backend
  - ○ Allow simple filtering by user name
  - ○ Provide editing capabilities for records
- Show user statistics in the BE:
  - ○ How many times a user has logged in
  - ○ When a user logged in the last time
  - ○ How much time a user has spent on the site
  - ○ What pages a user has visited, and how many times

Statistics parts will be modeled using the existing `loginusertrack` extension, but will be written from scratch because that extension is too old and does not use the new TYPO3 API.

Usability and Expandability

- The FE appearance must be easily customizable by website developers (both CSS and HTML)
- Extension should allow for adding new functions easily in future
- Extension should use both TypoScript and user-friendly FlexForm configuration
- Extension must be fully localizable

Technical

- Extension must work properly with cache.
- Extension must have developer's documentation and comments in the code.
- Extension will not consider query string when recording page statistics. Only the page ID is recorded.

Extension key

We will use `feuserstat` as an extension key. Such a key has several advantages:

- It is short but not too short
- It looks similar to an extension title
- It gives the user an idea of what the extension is about

To register an extension key, we created an account at the `typo3.org` website and registered a new key in the **Extension key** subsection of the **Extensions** section of the website. This key is now registered by the author of the book. The reader should not attempt to register it. Such attempts will fail. However, the user can use user_ feuserstart key if he/she wants to repeat all the coding himself/herself. Notice that the table and class names will change.

Frontend Plugins

Our extension is going to have one FE plugin. This plugin will perform two functions:

- Display user list
- Display single user information

The plugin will be cacheable. It will have clearly separate, reasonably sized methods. We should avoid code duplicates and write code so that it can be re-used by future functions.

One question that developers sometimes have to solve is how many plugins to make. For example, here, list and single views are placed in a single plugin. This increases the size of the PHP class and makes maintenance a little harder (solely because of the larger file). If list and single view go to separate plugins, they will be easier to maintain, but any common function will have to go to yet another common class, and the number of plugins will double. Two plugins will make a list of plugins in TYPO3 longer. Therefore, many extension authors choose to have a single plugin and several modes in it.

Yet another alternative to the many plugins is to make a separate class for each view.

Always consider these opportunities while planning plugins.

Backend Module

Our extension will have one BE module. It will perform functions from the requirements.

Other Classes

The extension needs a hook to catch when the following events happen in the system:

- User is logged in
- User is logged out
- User visits a page

We will research to find out which hooks we should use.

Extension Database Structure

Since we are going to work with FE users, we will use the `fe_users` standard TYPO3 table. We will not modify this table in any way. All our data will be stored in separate tables.

First, we need to store session information for users, such as session start, session end, and the number of visits during this session. Additionally, we will store the first and the last page visited during this session.

Next, for each session, we will record the number of hits per page. We will ignore query parameters for the page. It is important that we mention it here because it means we thought about this limitation at the planning stage. Query parameters may alter page content, and we choose to ignore them.

Records from both tables should be stored on the same page where FE user records are stored.

So, we will have two tables in the database. Let us plan them a little more.

The first table should have the following fields:

Field name	Field type	Description
uid	int	Standard TYPO3 field that uniquely identifies a record.
pid	int	Standard TYPO3 field that identifies the page where the records are located.
fe_user	int	This is the database relation to the `fe_users` table. We choose the integer field because we will reference only one table. We will need to specifically tell TYPO3 *not* to prefix a number to the table name.

Field name	Field type	Description
session_start	int	This is the Unix time stamp value of the time when the session starts.
session_end	int	This is the Unix time stamp value of the time when the session ends. We will update this value each time the user visits a page. Thus, the last value automatically becomes the time of the session end.
hits	int	The number of page hits for this session.
first_page	int	This is the database related to the pages table. It shows the page ID where the session started (user logged in).
last_page	int	This is the database related to the pages table. It shows the page ID where the session ended (user logged out or closed browser). It will be updated the same way as the session_end field.

The second table will have these fields:

Field name	Field type	Description
uid	int	Standard TYPO3 field that uniquely identifies a record.
pid	int	Standard TYPO3 field that identifies the page where the records are located.
crdate	int	Unix time stamp indicating the time when the record was created.
tstamp	int	Record's last updated Unix time stamp. This may seem to be overhead (because statistics are not meant to be modified). But this field will allow us to detect if any one changes statistics manually.
fe_user	int	This is a reference to the fe_users table.
sesstat_uid	int	This is a reference to the first table. Since it is the int field, we will tell TYPO3 not to prepend a number to the table name.
		We could use session ID as well, but it is preferable to have a relation between these two fields. TYPO3 will show users how many records from the second table are associated with the session recorded in the first table. We will have to maintain a reference index on the second table.

Field name	Field type	Description
page_uid	int	This is a relation to the pages table. It refers to a visited page.
hits	int	This field shows the number of hits for this page during a session.

Some readers may ask why we have hits field in both the tables. Can't we just have it in the second table, and use SQL SUM function to get a cumulative value? Yes, we can. But the SUM function is expensive in SQL when there are lots of records to select from therefore, we will use a dedicated field in the first table to count the number of visits per page.

Another issue we should take care of is to protect these tables from manual modifications by the BE users.

We also recognize that the chosen database structure does not allow us to trace user navigation across the site.

We will not define database indexes now. We will define them when we build queries. The table names will be defined when we generate the extension.

Documentation

Besides normal extension description, the extension manual should include information on clearing the page cache to ensure that the list shows updated information when a new user record is added to the list.

Summary

In this chapter, we have seen how important extension planning is. We reviewed some basic principles of extension planning, saw TYPO3-specific issues, and talked about database structure. We also planned our own extension, which we will develop later in this book.

Generating Extensions

In this chapter, we will create a skeleton for our extension. Later, it will be adjusted to better fit our needs. After completing this chapter, the reader should be able to generate new extensions easily.

Why Generation?

TYPO3 extensions can be created manually. We already know which files are needed and which functions should be called to add Frontend plugins or Backend modules. So, why should we generate an extension instead of simply typing it out?

Although typing is perfectly valid, it is slow. It requires one to concentrate on the content. Typing errors are likely unless the extension developer uses a modern PHP IDE (such as Zend Studio). It is easy to forget something if an extension has several modules and tables.

Extension generation has several other advantages over the manual creation of extensions. Firstly, a developer can really concentrate on the extension details, not on putting these details into various files. Secondly, generation process ensures that all files are created, all modules are added, and all links between tables are established properly. And thirdly, it simply saves a lot of time for the developers.

Preparing for Generation

Generation of an extension is performed inside TYPO3 BE by another extension named Kickstarter (extension key: `kickstarter`). This extension should be downloaded and installed to TYPO3 like any other extension (through the TYPO3 Extension Manager). Once installed, a new item named **Make new extension** appears in the Extension Manager functions:

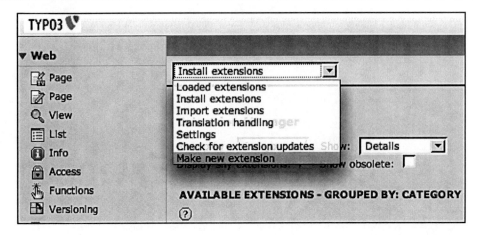

The official version of Kickstarter is updated rarely. Assuming that the current directory is the TYPO3 root directory, a newer (but possibly unstable) version can be obtained from SourceForge SVN using the following SVN command within a shell prompt:

```
svn co https://typo3xdev.svn.sourceforge.net/svnroot/typo3xdev/tx_
kickstarter/trunk typo3conf/ext/kickstarter
```

The author of this book uses the SVN version of Kickstarter because it has several bug fixes, is more compatible with TYPO3 coding conventions, and uses the most recent TYPO3 API.

Generation Steps

Extension generation consists of several steps. Some of them are optional, while some are mandatory. There is always a start step that must be performed before any other. Failing to do it will result in an incorrectly generated extension. This section will describe each step in detail. But first, we need to get familiar with the Kickstarter user interface. It is recommended to perform each step while reading.

The Kickstarter user interface is fairly simple. It consists of the steps on the left side of the screen and information area on the right. When a new step is reached on the left, the information area on the right changes. Kickstarter looks like this when **Make new extension** is selected in TYPO3 Extension Manager:

```
KICKSTARTER WIZARD
General info                      +
Setup languages                   +
New Database Tables               +
Extend existing Tables            +
Frontend Plugins                  +
Backend Modules                   +
Integrate in existing Modules  +
Clickmenu items                   +
Services                          +
Static TypoScript code            +
TSconfig                          +


Enter extension key:
[                    ]
Make sure to enter the right
extension key from the
beginning here! You can register
one here.
[ Update... ]
[ Total form ]
```

Entering an Extension key

This step must be performed first, and it is extremely important to generate an extension correctly. If you performed any other step, there is no way to go back and change the extension key; you will have to start everything from the beginning. Kickstarter caches information as soon as you start performing the steps. So, if you created a plugin and then decided to change the key, the plugin class name will not be updated with a new key and you will get an error in the generated extension.

To enter an extension key, navigate to the input field below the steps, enter an extension key (feuserstat in our case) and click the **Update...** button.

The **Total form** button below **Update...** shows a complete form for all the steps at one time. It will be very long and not too useful.

Entering Extension Information

The next step is to enter extension information. To do this, click on the black plus icon to the right of the **General info** step.

The following fields are available:

Field	Description
Title	This is the extension's title as shown by TYPO3 Extension Repository (TER) and TYPO3 Extension Manager (EM).
Description	This is the extension's description as shown by TER and EM.
Category	This is the extension's category. In our case, the extension included both the **Frontend plugin** and **Backend module**. There is no category for this case so we just arbitrarily choose **Frontend plugins**.
State	This is a state of the extension. We will keep it as **Alpha (Very initial development)** for now.
Dependencies	As there are no dependencies on other extensions in our extension, we will leave this field blank.
Author Name	Extension author name.
Author email	Extension author email ID.

We will fill the above explained fields as shown in the following screenshot:

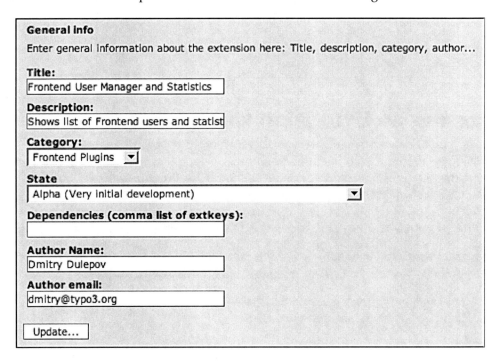

To finish this step, press the **Update...** button.

Set Up Languages

This section shows how to set up additional languages. This is useful when you want to add nondefault (non-English) labels to an extension. However, note that it is discouraged to have labels for a nondefault language directly in an extension. All such labels should be extracted and packaged as a part of TYPO3 language packs when an extension is released to TER. For information on moving language labels to TYPO3 language packs, see the TYPO3 Wiki at `http://wiki.typo3.org/index.php/Translation`.

This is how this step looks in Kickstarter:

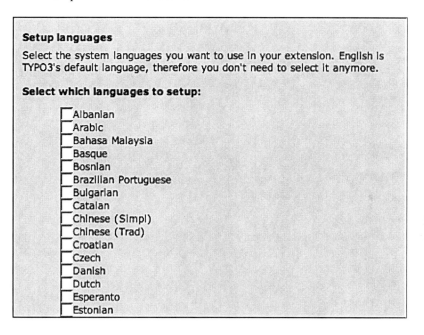

To add languages, simply check the appropriate checkboxes and click the **Update...** button.

Creating New Database Tables

This is one of the most important steps. Here, we will define database tables for the extension. In this step, we will click on the black plus icon, once for each table. We will create two tables for our extension. But first we will talk about options that this step provides for creating tables. Since there are a lot of options, we will discuss them in groups.

The first group of options provides generic information about the table: title, description, hidden and deleted flags, start and stop time, Frontend groups, and so on. This is how these options look:

If an extension developer has selected additional languages in the second step, there will be additional input fields (one per language) below the **Title of the table** field.

All options (except the last one) on this screen have already been discussed in the previous chapters. The Deleted field is set to 1 in the database when a record is deleted. The Hidden field hides a record in the Frontend. Starttime and endtime define a period when a record is visible (empty means no limit on the side). The last option on this screenshot (named Access group) adds a field to the table that stores relations, the fe_groups table. This allows us to restrict access to data from this table for certain visitors. This field will be visible in the BE form, and the corresponding additions to the SQL WHERE statement will be available in the Frontend plugins automatically through the API function (tslib_cObj::enableFields). We will see how to use all these access fields in Chapter 5 and 6.

Note that Kickstarter will generate start and end times as the palette attached to the `Hidden` field. Palettes usually do not appear on the screen unless an editor presses the icon to the right of the corresponding field.

The next group of options is shown in the following image:

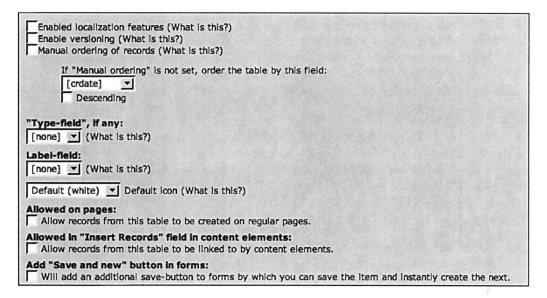

Here, Kickstarter combines several logically different options. The first two define the behavior of the table, while the rest define its visual presentation.

If localization is enabled for the table, it becomes possible to store translations of the table's records inside the same table using a set of special fields. Generally, these fields say which record is the main one and which ones are language dependent. There are certain other fields, but we will not discuss TYPO3 localization details here. This topic is so large that it could easily take an entire chapter. Those who want to read more about localization should read the **Frontend localization guide** document on the typo3.org website. We, however, will have a short discussion about selecting records for the current Frontend language in Chapter 5.

The **Enable versioning** box allows us to add versioning support for a table. Versioning support is another tricky part of TYPO3. While it is used by many in production, it is still considered to be of beta quality. We will not use it in our extension.

Manual ordering of records allows BE users to order records manually, for example, pages or content elements. If this box is not checked, automatic sorting is applied to records (it defaults to record creation time).

Type-field is another powerful but tricky feature of TYPO3 tables. Each table may have such a field. This field defines what a record truly is. For example, the tt_news extension defines three types for news items: normal news, link to an internal page, and link to an external page. A form may show different set of fields depending on the **Type-field**. This is often better than making separate tables for slightly different data. Additionally, the type fields allow to show different icons for records in the **List** module. If a developer uses the type field, he/she must remember that Kickstarter will generate default table configuration, where all fields are available. It is the developer's responsibility to review the types configuration for the table later and adjust the displayed field set. More information on type fields and how to use them can be found in the **TYPO3 Core API** document on the typo3.org website.

A developer can specify which field should present a record in the **List** module using **Label-field**. TYPO3 treats the value of this field as a "personal name" of the record. Sometimes, it is not possible to set one field (or any field at all) as a **label** field. In this case, an extension developer should read the **['ctrl'] section** under the **$TCA array reference** heading from the **TYPO3 Core API** document. This section explains how to combine several fields into a **label** field or write a custom PHP function to return the label.

The default icon selector can be left as it is. Typically, developers find or create icons for their tables at some point in development. Values in these fields are meant only to generate some stock icons for table records.

The **Allowed on pages** option will allow records from this table to be created on normal pages. For records such as statistics or logs, this option should not be selected. However, for records such as news or products, this option should be selected. TYPO3 will refuse to create records for the table in the BE on regular pages, if this option is not checked.

The next option, **Allowed in "Insert Records" field in content elements**, is rarely used. It allows us to insert records from this table as content elements.

The option to **Add "Save and new" button in forms** is very useful for records that should be added one after another. A good example is news articles – one often has to fill more than one news item. If this box is checked, an additional icon appears in the BE form for the record:

Now, go to the field descriptions. Initially, the form for field description consists of three fields:

```
NEW FIELD:
Field name: [                              ]
Field title: [                           ] [English]
Field type:  [                        ▼][✓] Is Exclude-field (What is this?)
```

Field name is the name of the field in a database. Notice that Kickstarter will not check if a field name is a reserved SQL keyword. So, if a developer attempts to use "index" or "date" as a database field name, MySQL will throw errors while creating a table. This Kickstarter behavior may be fixed in future.

Field title is a string visible in the BE form for the field. Make sure to put a colon as the last character. If additional languages were selected on the corresponding step, this field will have additional fields below it for each selected language.

Field type defines what information will be stored in this field. This is not SQL field type but TYPO3 type field. It is very important to select the type properly here because Kickstarter will generate lots of code lines depending on this selection.

The available field types are listed in the following table.

Field type	Description	SQL types
String input	Creates a simple string. Any character can be entered.	tinytext
String input, advanced	Creates a string but allows us to impose certain limitations (no space, alpha numeric) and apply conversions (trim, integer) to the string in the BE form.	text varchar
Text area Text area with RTE Text area, no wrapping	Creates a text area. Name of the type says how exactly the text area will be created.	text

Field type	Description	SQL types
Checkbox single Checkbox, 4 boxes in a row Checkbox, 10 boxes in two rows (max)	Creates a checkbox or a set of checkboxes. These three options are here only to simplify a developer's work. They allow us to make initial arrangements for checkboxes that developers can alter as they need. Notice that "max" in the last option applies to this option only, not to the number of checkboxes that TYPO3 may have. However, a developer must check the length of the integer field in the ext_table.sql after extension generation. By default, it is int(11), which means that this field can hold up to 11 check boxes (1 bit = 1 checkbox).	int
Link	Links field. This is just a string field in the database but TYPO3 provides a special control for it (with link wizard) and makes certain conventions on this field depending on the link type (internal page, external link, email, file, and so on)	varchar
Date Date and time	These fields are similar and differ only in how TYPO3 BE shows them. There is no "time" type, but a developer can easily add it if necessary after studying how "date" fields are defined. Date and time fields are stored as Unix time stamps in the database.	int
Integer, 10-100	This is a simple integer field. Again, as with checkboxes, 10-100 is the artificial limitation here. It is made only to show a developer how to impose range limitations on integers. It can easily be changed by editing the tca.php file after extension generation.	int
Selector box	This is a simple selector box of values. This field is typically used for type fields (see above about type fields). Kickstarter will allow the developer to enter up to 10 values and generates numerical indexes for values. If a developer wants string indexes, he can modify tca.php and ext_tables.sql later on to use string values as indexes. In this case, SQL field type should be changed to varchar or text.	int

Field type	Description	SQL types
Radio buttons	This type represents a set of radio buttons. The number of selected buttons (counting from 0) is stored in the database.	int
Database relation	This type represents the database relation inside TYPO3. It is possible to create relations between an extension's own tables and a table in the system.	text
	If two tables are related to each other, then create the first table with a relation field and leave the relation empty. Next, create the second table and fill its relation information properly. Now, go back to the first table and select the second table instead of the empty value in the earlier created field.	
	While creating this field, pay attention to the following moments.	
	When deciding what to use (selector box or relations control), think about the number of items. A Selector box with hundred items is not a good solution, an element browser will definitely be better. However, if a user should select from a list of web site languages, a selector box is better than an element browser.	
	The number of items in the relation should be specified according to the extension needs. There are extensions that need only one item, but give the option to select many. This confuses editors.	
	It is possible to add additional control to add, edit, or list records. While they look good, controls should not be added only because they look good. There should be a definite use case to have these controls in the form.	
Inline relation	Inline relations are tricky and Kickstarter has certain bugs in the implementation of inline relations. Use this type only if you know how inline relations work.	Many fields of int and varchar type
	Warning: At the time of writing this book, this choice was available only in the SVN version of Kickstarter, and its implementation has certain bugs. Do not use this option unless you feel capable of fixing errors with IRRE structures manually.	

Field type	Description	SQL types
Files	File control is similar to database relations. An extension developer can choose which files to include, how many files to allow, and the maximum file size.	text
Flex	This field type is for experienced extension developers. It is used to create a flexform. Flexform is a TYPO3 way to have one form inside another form. Flexforms store value in a single database field in an XML format. The t3lib_div::xml2array() function should be used to convert XML to a PHP array.	text
	Information about flexforms can be found in the TYPO3 Core API document on the typo3.org website. We will discuss flexforms and create a simple flexform while developing Frontend plugin later in this book.	
Not editable, only displayed	A value from the database will be passed to the htmlspecialchars() PHP function and then directly to the form. This field is generated but should not be changed by an editor in the BE. A similar effect can be achieved with String input fields by setting the readOnly property for these fields in $TCA (see **TYPO3 Core API**). The input field has an advantage because they can be shown as dates (for example).	text
[Passthrough]	This is for the field that should be created in the database but not shown in the form.	text

After modifying the field data, press the **Update...** button to save field changes. It is possible to modify one field and create another at the same time. Kickstarter will save all changes in the form when **Update...** is pressed.

We already discussed which fields we will have in Chapter 3. Now, let's see how we can configure them in Kickstarter.

The first table will be named tx_feuserstat_sessions. The title for the table will be **Frontend user sessions**. It will have the following fields:

Field	ConfigurationTitle
fe_user	Database relation to the fe_users table with element browser, single item in the control.
session_start	String input, advanced. We make it required, 15 symbols in size. Field evaluates to date and time.

Field	ConfigurationTitle
session_end	String input, advanced. We make it required, 15 symbols in size. Field evaluates to date and time.
hits	Integer value, 10-100. We will remove limits later.
first_page	Database reference to the pages table with element browser, single element in the control.
last_page	Database reference to the pages table with element browser, single element in the control.

Note that normally table titles should be singular. This is due to the fact that the List module will use the table name when a new record is created. In our case, it does not make a big difference because our tables will be hidden in the BE. Therefore, we name them logically.

There are no hidden, deleted, starttime, endtime, or Frontend group fields in the table. We will also mark the table as read-only later so that no one is able to change the statistics.

The second table will be named tx_feuserstat_pagestats. The title is **Page statistics**, and the table will have the following configuration:

Field	Title	Configuration
fe_user	**Frontend user:**	Database relation to the fe_users table with element browser, single item in the control.
sesstat_uid	**Session:**	Database relation to the tx_feuserstat_sessions table with element browser, single item in the control.
page_uid	**Visited page:**	Database relation to the pages table with element browser, single item in the control.
hits	**Visits:**	Integer value is 10-100. We will remove the limits later.

This table will also have no deleted, hidden, or other access related fields. This table will also be marked as read-only to prevent manipulation of statistics.

Extending Existing Tables

Sometimes it is necessary to extend existing tables. For example, some extensions add custom fields to content elements (such as extension rgmediaimages) or to the tt_news table (such as ratings extension). While it is possible to have such data separately, it is much easier and more practical to add it to the existing tables. Additions, for example, allow to edit these fields together with the extended record, which would not be possible if fields were created as a separate table.

Kickstarter allows to extend existing tables. It proposes to choose tables first. A table must exist in the TYPO3 database already. The rest is similar to creating a new table; all the same field types, the same workflow.

There is one special thing though. All extended tables must be listed in the `modify_tables` option of the `ext_emconf.php` file. Kickstarter does not put extended tables into this entry automatically, and it has to be done manually by the extension developer. If not done, the Extension Manager will complain about it:

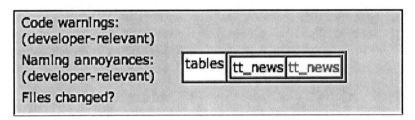

While this is not critical for extension functioning, it makes a bad impression on the extension. Do not forget to add modified tables to `modify_tables` in `ext_emconf.php`!

We will not have any extended tables in our extension.

Creating Frontend Plugins

The Frontend plugin step will allow us to create several plugins if necessary. We planned only one plugin for our extension.

All options in this step are important to get the Frontend plugin created correctly. Here is how the top part of this step looks:

Frontend Plugins

Create frontend plugins. Plugins are web applications running on the website itself (not in the backend of TYPO3). The default guestbook, message board, shop, rating feature etc. are examples of plugins.

Enter a title for the plugin:

[   ] [English]

☐ By default plugins are generated as cachable USER cObjects. Check this checkbox to generate an uncached USER_INT cObject.

☐ Enable this option if you want the TypoScript code to be set by default. Otherwise the code will go into a static template file which must be included in the template record (It's *NOT* recommended to set this option).

The title of the plugin will be visible in the BE when an editor inserts the plugin as a content element to the page. Therefore, it should be descriptive but not too long. It will be shown in the selector box of the `tt_content` item:

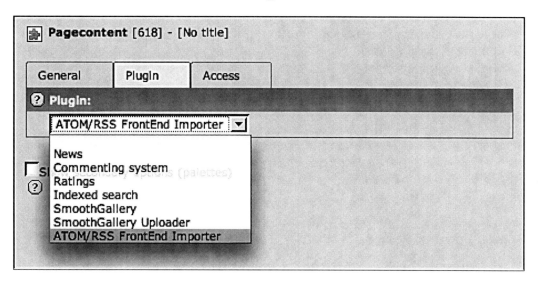

We will use **Frontend user list** as the plugin title.

The next option affects the performance of the TYPO3 website. Frontend plugins can be cacheable or noncacheable. Cacheable plugins are faster; their output is saved to the database with the rest of the page content once, and later all website visitors see this cached copy. So, no PHP code of the plugin needs to be executed. This works fine for static or rarely changing data.

Some plugins show information depending on user input, or generate quickly changing data (real time stock reports, web server performance statistics, and so on). There is no point in caching this output. So, such plugins should not be cacheable.

Caching should also be avoided for many (but not all) plugins that process user input. For example, if a plugin validates information before adding it to the database, it may produce error messages, which should not be cached. Such plugins do not do much processing unless the form is submitted, so it is perfectly fine to make them noncacheable.

Yet another case when the plugins have to be noncacheable is when they gather information about user visits. For example, the `ttnews_reads` extension has a plugin that is inserted before the `tt_news` single view plugin. It does not produce any output, but augments the view counter for each viewed news item. As this plugin has to be executed each time a news item is displayed, it must not be cacheable.

So, the question of caching is very important for a Frontend plugin. The general rule is, if a developer can make it cacheable while keeping all functionalities, then the plugin should be cacheable.

In our case, we will have a search box in the user list mode. However, there will be no validation and error messages from this search box. It will simply act as a filter. Therefore, we should probably use caching. But how can we use caching if a user is allowed to type anything in the search box? Based on the above information, such input should not be cached.

Fortunately, TYPO3 may cache various copies of data depending on user input. While it does not make any sense to cache error messages, caching such inputs makes perfect sense. Therefore, we will choose a cacheable plugin. We will see later how we can ensure proper caching for our plugin. There is certain cost associated with it, but this cost is not large when compared to the performance impact of a noncacheable plugin.

The next option adds the TypoScript template permanently to TYPO3. This should be avoided because it forces TYPO3 to parse more TypoScript and makes TYPO3 performance worse.

Next, there is a set of choices for the Frontend plugin type. Depending on the selected options, Kickstarter will generate different codes for the plugin and call different TYPO3 functions to add the plugin to TYPO3. These options are well described in Kickstarter. It is possible to create a normal plugin (this is the most typical choice), text box (obsolete), menu/sitemap (Google sitemap extensions use this), totally new content element, header type, process tag in RTE, or to simply include the library.

The normal Frontend plugin can have an option to be included in the new content element wizard.

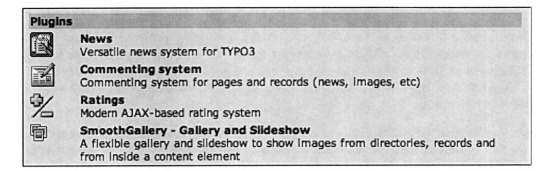

Generally, this option should not be set. However, if an extension is made for a specific customer (not a public extension), it is preferable to set this option because it will be easier for the customer to use it. However, we will not set this option for our plugin.

One special plugin case is "totally new content element". It is very similar to a normal plugin but it allows a developer to define a custom content object in TypoScript. By default, all normal plugins are USER or USER_INT objects. Defining new types makes the following possible in TypoScript setup:

```
page.10 = FLASH
page.10.source = /fileadmin/myfile.swf
page.10.clickTag = http://domain.com/
```

Here, a new content object of type FLASH is defined. All properties are specific to this object. TYPO3 will call the plugin passing all objects' TypoScript properties. Also, the plugin will be shown as a separate content element type. These are really the only differences from a normal plugin.

We will use the first choice for our plugin: **Add to 'Insert Plugin' list in Content Elements**.

Creating Backend Modules

This step generates BE modules. As with Frontend plugins, it is possible to generate more than one module by clicking the plus icon more than once.

BE modules can be generated as main modules (examples are **Web**, **File**, **User Tools**, **Admin Tools**) or as submodules (examples are **Web | Page** and **User | Setup**). It is not recommended to create main modules because too many of them will make the TYPO3 menu very long.

While deciding where to create a submodule, think what the module will need. If it needs a page ID, it should go to the **Web** module. If it works with files and directories, it should be a part of the **File** module. If it does not need page ID or the current directory, it should go to the **User** (available to anyone) or the **Tools** (admin-only) module.

Our module needs a page ID because it will show statistics only for Frontend user records at a specific page. Therefore, we will place it in the **Web** module after the **Info** submodule. We will call our BE module "Frontend user statistics". Its description will be "Shows Frontend user session and page view statistics". A shorter description can be "FE statistics".

Integrating into Existing Modules

This step allows us to integrate a new module into an existing module. We could choose to do so and use **Web | Info** as our parent module. But for the purpose of the book, we will make it a separate module.

Adding Clickmenu Items

This step allows us to add an item to a TYPO3 click menu. A click menu appears when an editor clicks on the icons in the BE. Its contents depend on the context. Kickstarter will generate code that adds a menu item and a handler for the menu item.

As usual, this should be used with care. Too many menu items will not be appreciated by the editors.

Creating Services

This step allows us to create services. We discussed services in the previous chapters. It is a rare that a new service is needed, and we will not cover services in this book. Therefore, we will skip this step completely. Developers interested in services can find the documentation about services in the **Documentation** section of the typo3.org website. There are also several extensions that implement services. They can be used as examples.

Static TypoScript Code

This step allows us to enter plugin TypoScript configuration. There are two parts of TypoScript code: **Constants** and **Setup**. Constants can be easily edited with TYPO3 Constant Editor in **Web | Template** module and it is strongly recommended to define the constants for the most commonly used TypoScript setup parameters.

The TypoScript template title will be **Frontend user list**, and we will start filling the TypoScript parameters from the Setup part. We will add constants later.

First, we need to define the plugin. Plugin names are generated by appending several parts to one string:

- `plugin.tx_`
- extension key without underscores
- `_pi`X suffix, where X is the number of plugins starting from 1

Therefore, our Frontend plugin will appear in the setup as `plugin.tx_feuserstat_pi1`. It will have USER type and we will add several basic TypoScript properties to it. More properties can be added later, if necessary. We will enter the following in the **Setup** part:

```
plugin.tx_feuserstat_pi1 = USER
plugin.tx_feuserstat_pi1 {
    # uid of the page where Frontend user records are stored
    usersPid = {$plugin.tx_feuserstat_pi1.usersPid}
    # uid of the page where single view is located
    singlePid = {$plugin.tx_feuserstat_pi1.singlePid}
    # uid of the page where list view is located
    listPid = {$plugin.tx_feuserstat_pi1.listPid}
    # Template file to use
    templateFile = {$plugin.tx_feuserstat_pi1.templateFile}
}
```

Lines with # are comments.

First, we should have a place to save our records. Since there can be many sites in a single TYPO3 installation, we will want to collect statistics for each site separately. Therefore, we need a "storage" page.

For the same reason, we also need to know where the Frontend users are placed in TYPO3. So, we have a configuration for Frontend user storage.

Our plugin will have a list of single views, and these views may be placed on different pages. We definitely need a link to a single view from the list view and we may want to create a backward link. So, we have two more configuration settings for the list and single page ID values.

The last option declares the location of the template file for our plugin. We will provide a default template, but a website designer may want to replace our template with his own. We will make it easy by allowing him/her to place the template file into `fileadmin/` and tell our plugin about it through this configuration setting.

The USER_INT plugins must have one more line in the TS setup declaring where the plugin is located. The reason for this is simple: USER_INT plugins are included by TYPO3 directly, bypassing normal TypoScript processing. Without this additional part, TYPO3 will not be able to find the plugin. If our plugin was USER_INT, we would have added the following to the TypoScript setup of the plugin on the third line:

```
includeLibs = EXT:feuserstat/pi1/class.tx_feuserstat_pi1.php
```

Now, we have a setup section and we should fill the constants.

Constants are similar to setups, except that they have initial values and special comments. Comments declare how a constant editor will show constants to a user. The syntax of such comments was described in Chapter 2.

We enter the following in constants:

```
plugin.tx_feuserstat_pi1 {
    # cat=feuserstat; type=int+; label=User storage page:
uid of the page where Frontend user records are stored
    usersPid =
    # cat=feuserstat; type=int+; label=Single view page:
uid of the page where single view is located
    singlePid =
    # cat=feuserstat; type=int+; label=List view page:
uid of the page where list view is located
    listPid =
    # cat=feuserstat; type=string; label=Template file
    templateFile = EXT:feuserstat/res/pi1_template.html
}
```

Most of the values are empty because we cannot predict page uid values. We supply a default value for the plugin template as a reference to the file inside the extension. Note that the comment for the template file does not have the second part for the label. It is obvious what this setting means without further explanation.

Adding TSConfig

Sometimes, extensions need to alter BE behavior in a certain way. For example, an extension developer may want to hide one or more extension tables or provide default TSConfig for his/her own modules. This step allows us to enter TSConfig code that is appended to default code for the user and the page.

Information about TSConfig syntax and features can be found in the **TSConfig** document in the **Documentation** section of the typo3.org website.

We will not have any additions to TSConfig in our extension.

Generating the Extension

Now, we are ready to generate our extension. Clicking the **View result** button shows us the following overview:

Filename:	Size:		Overwrite:
ChangeLog	90		☑
README.txt	80	View	☑
ext_icon.gif	124		☑
ext_localconf.php	159	View	☑
ext_tables.php	0.9 K	View	☑
ext_tables.sql	399	View	☑
icon_tx_feusermgr.gif	135		☑
locallang_db.xml	381	View	☑
tca.php	1.0 K	View	☑
doc/wizard_form.dat	2.1 K		
doc/wizard_form.html	48 K		
mod1/clear.gif	46		☑
mod1/conf.php	358	View	☑
mod1/index.php	6.8 K	View	☑
mod1/locallang.xml	459	View	☑
mod1/locallang_mod.xml	275	View	☑
mod1/moduleicon.gif	82		☑
pi1/class.tx_feusermgr_pi1.php	2.8 K	View	☑
pi1/locallang.xml	558	View	☑

[Update result]

Author name: Dmitry Dulepov
Author email: dmitry@typo3.org

Write to location:
[Local: typo3conf/ext/feusermgr/ (empty) ▼] [WRITE]

We will uncheck the **README.txt** option because this file does not contain anything useful and click **Update result**. Next, we click the **WRITE** button. Kickstarter will write extension files to the disk. Make sure that a web server user can write into the shown location before clicking **WRITE**.

We just finished generating our extension! Now let's see what we have got and we will adjust some generated code.

Adjusting Extensions

After generation, we will make adjustments to our generated extension according to our needs.

Clean Up

Firstly, if we are sure that we generated the extension correctly, we should go and remove two files named `wizard_form.dat` and `wizard_form.html` from the `doc/` subdirectory. These files contain Kickstarter information. It is possible to use Kickstarter to reconfigure extension. However, any manual changes in files will be completely lost.

Changing Fields

The next thing to do is to change `tca.php` to remove limits from the integer fields. The following lines should be removed from both the generated tables in the `hits` column:

```
'range' => array (
    'upper' => '1000',
    'lower' => '10'
),
```

Next, we update the `fe_user` field in both the tables, `first_page` and `last_page` in the first table, `sesstat_uid` and `page_uid` in the second table and `minitems` should be set to `1`.

Now, we need to optimize SQL fields. We do so by changing `ext_tables.sql`. We will change `fe_user`, `first_page`, `last_page`, `sesstat_uid`, and `page_uid` fields from text to `int(11) DEFAULT '0' NOT NULL`.

Hide Tables

Now, we need to hide our tables to prevent anyone from changing statistics. To hide our tables, we open `ext_tables.php` and add the following line:

```
'hideTable' => true,
```

This line should be added twice (once for each table) after this line:

```
'default_sortby' => 'ORDER BY crdate',
```

This concludes our changes to the generated extension.

Summary

In this chapter, we learned about extension generation and generated an extension that we will develop through this book. Now, we know a lot about extensions and how to generate them in an optimal way. We know how to use TYPO3 data types effectively and how to adjust generated fields after generation.

In the forthcoming chapters, we will look deeper into the extension parts and continue with practical extension development.

5

Frontend Plugin: An In-Depth Study

Frontend plugin is the most popular extension component type in TYPO3 extension development. Frontend plugins can do many things: they can create content, modify existing content, log statistics, and so on. They are simple to write; only a few lines are needed to create the simplest Frontend plugin. But creating a good plugin requires certain knowledge. This chapter discusses Frontend plugins in detail. It also discusses many other functions to use with Frontend plugins.

Frontend Plugins: The Basics

This section will describe the basics of the Frontend plugins. The main goal of this section is to give the reader an overview and basic understanding of what Frontend plugins are, how they work, and what they look like. The details are discussed later in this chapter.

Concepts

A Frontend plugin is a class or a function that runs as a part of the page content generation process. Typically, Frontend plugins produce some visible content, but they can also be silent and do other tasks.

The simplest possible Frontend plugin looks like this:

```
function user_myext_plugin() {
    return 'Hello world!';
}
```

To call such a plugin, use the following TypoScript:

```
includeLibs.myext_plugin = EXT:myext/user_myext_plugin.php
page.10 = USER
page.10.userFunc = user_myext_plugin
```

The first line includes the PHP file with a plugin code. The second line defines that the plugin type is USER. There are several types of plugins. USER is the most common and it means that the plugin's output is cached by TYPO3. Caching issues will be covered later in this chapter. The third line tells TYPO3 which function to execute for this plugin. The function name must start with user_, otherwise, TYPO3 will not call it. For classes, the corresponding prefix is tx_.

While it is possible to create Frontend plugins this way (and sometimes it is even more optimal to call PHP code this way), typically, Frontend plugins are created as classes. The advantages of using classes are:

- Classes can have functions to split long code into logical, easily readable, and maintainable chunks.
- Classes can encapsulate data inside class instances and use this data in class functions.
- Classes can derive from other classes and reuse their methods.

The Kickstarter extension generates Frontend plugins as classes derived from the tslib_pibase class. The generated class looks approximately like this (assuming myext as an extension key):

```
class tx_myext_pi1 extends tslib_pibase {
    // Default plugin variables:
    var $prefixId = 'tx_myext_pi1';
    var $scriptRelPath = 'pi1/class.tx_myext_pi1.php';
    var $extKey = 'myext';
    var $pi_checkCHash = true;
    /**
     * The main method of the PlugIn
     *
     * @param    string         $content: The PlugIn content
     * @param    array          $conf: The PlugIn configuration
     * @return   The content that is displayed on the website
     */
    function main($content, $conf) {
        $this->conf = $conf;
        $this->pi_setPiVarDefaults();
        $this->pi_loadLL();
        $content = 'Dummy content';
        return $this->pi_wrapInBaseClass($content);
    }
}
```

There are additional lines in the generated file but there is no need to look at them now. First of all, let's see what Kickstarter generates.

Kickstarter creates a class named `tx_myext_pi1` and places it into a directory named `pi1` inside the extension. This class is derived from the `tslib_pibase` class. The `tslib_pibase` class should be treated as an abstract class, and should never be instantiated directly. It is possible that the future versions of TYPO3 will add the `abstract` keyword to the `tslib_pibase` definition.

The `tslib_pibase` class contains functions that Frontend plugins frequently use: loading localized strings, creating links, and fetching flexform configuration information.

To work correctly, the `tslib_pibase` class requires three class variables to be set correctly. They are set on the first three lines inside the plugin's class.

The last class variable generated by Kickstarter is named `$pi_checkCHash`. It instructs TYPO3 to validate `cHash`, which is a special URL parameter inside the `tslib_pibase` constructor. The `cHash` parameter is related to the caching of the page that has parameters. It is discussed in a separate section of this chapter due to its extreme importance for Frontend plugins.

Next comes the definition of the plugin's `main()` function. While plugins are not required to use this name, it has traditionally been used, and it is recommended to follow this tradition.

The function assigns the plugin configuration to a class variable, sets default plugin variables from TypoScript (rarely used), and loads localized strings from the `locallang.xml` file onto the plugin's directory. Now, the plugin can use the `$this->pi_getLL('string_id')` function to load localized strings. We will discuss localization again, later in this chapter, as it is important.

The last line of `main()` contains a call to `pi_wrapInBaseClass`, which wraps output of the extension into `div` tags with CSS class derived from the extension key (`tx-myext-pi1` in our example). It is important to keep this call because it provides a generic and useful way to style the whole plugin.

This plugin can be executed from TypoScript in the following way:

```
page.10 = USER
page.10.userFunc = tx_myext_pi1->main
```

This will call the `main()` function of the plugin. TYPO3 usually passes an empty string to the `$content` parameter (the first one) and values from TypoScript setup in `$conf` (the second one).

Plugin Configuration

There are two ways to configure a plugin. TypoScript configuration is always available to the plugin, regardless of how it is inserted into the page (either through TypoScript or through an **Insert plugin** option on content element record). The Flexform configuration is available only when the plugin is inserted using the **Insert plugin** option.

TypoScript Configuration

It is possible to pass configuration values to the extension from TypoScript:

```
page.10 = USER
page.10 {
    userFunc = tx_myext_pi1->main
    param = value
}
```

With this piece of TypoScript, the `main()` function will receive the `$conf` parameter, which is an array with two keys, `userFunc` and `param`. The corresponding values are `tx_myext_pi1->main` and `value`.

If an extension developer entered TypoScript code in the Kickstarter as we had discussed in Chapter 4, it is possible to reuse the entered code:

```
page.10 < plugin.tx_myext_pi1 = USER
page.10.param = value
```

In this case, the plugin receives all the configuration values from its default TypoScript setup (made with Kickstarter) and possibly the modified value of `param`.

Flexform Configuration

Flexform is a good way to let a plugin present complex configuration forms without creating many additional fields in the database. TYPO3 stores flexform data in a single, already existing database field in an XML format. Here is what flexform looks like (example from the `comments` extension):

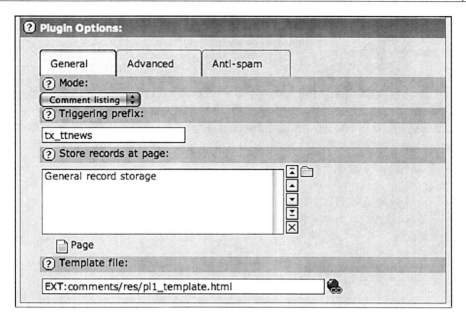

Unfortunately, Kickstarter does not generate a flexform and the code to process it yet. It has to be done manually.

To use a flexform in the plugin, it has to be initialized first:

```
$this->pi_initPIflexForm();
```

This line should be placed somewhere after the following line:

```
$this->pi_loadLL();
```

When the flexform is initialized, it is possible to get the value from the flexform using the following code:

```
$value = $this->pi_getFFvalue(
            $this->cObj->data['pi_flexform'],
            $paramName, $sheetName);
```

The `$sheetName` variable can be omitted if there is only one sheet in the flexform. Each sheet is rendered as a tab in the user interface. For example, the previous screenshot has three tabs and three sheets in the flexform definition.

It is good practice to define defaults in the TypoScript and allow editors to modify them using a flexform. For example:

```
$value = $this->conf['storagePid'];
$ffValue = $this->pi_getFFvalue(
            $this->cObj->data['pi_flexform'],
```

```
                            'storagePid');
    if ($ffValue) {
        $value = $ffValue;
    }
```

To create a configuration for flexform (called "flexform data source"), an XML file should be created in the extension directory. It is suggested to place it in the same directory where the Frontend plugin resides. Here is an example of such a file (from ratings extension):

```
<T3DataStructure>
    <meta>
        <langDisable>1</langDisable>
        <langChildren>0</langChildren>
    </meta>
    <ROOT>
        <type>array</type>
        <el>
          <storagePid>
                <TCEforms>
                    <label>LLL:EXT:ratings/pi1/locallang.xml:
tt_content.tx_ratings_pi1.storage.page</label>
                    <config>
                        <type>group</type>
                        <internal_type>db</internal_type>
                        <allowed>pages</allowed>
                        <prepand_tname>0</prepand_tname>
                        <multiple>0</multiple>
                        <minitems>0</minitems>
                        <maxitems>1</maxitems>
                        <size>1</size>
                    </config>
                </TCEforms>
            </storagePid>
            <templateFile>
                <TCEforms>
                    <label>LLL:EXT:ratings/pi1/locallang.xml:
tt_content.tx_ratings_pi1.template_file</label>
                    <config>
                        <type>input</type>
                        <eval>trim,required</eval>
                        <default>
EXT:ratings/res/pi1_template.html</default>
                        <wizards type="array">
                            <_PADDING>2</_PADDING>
```

```
                     <link type="array">
                        <type>popup</type>
                        <title>Link</title>
                        <icon>link_popup.gif</icon>
                        <script>browse_links.php?
mode=wizard&amp;act=file</script>
                        <params type="array">
                           <blindLinkOptions>
page,url,mail,spec</blindLinkOptions>
                        </params>
                        <JSopenParams>
height=300,width=500,status=0,menubar=0,scrollbars=1</JSopenParams>
                     </link>
                  </wizards>
               </config>
            </TCEforms>
         </templateFile>
      </el>
   </ROOT>
</T3DataStructure>
```

This flexform defines two fields: `storagePid` and `templateFile`. Tags inside a field definition correspond to the field definitions in `$TCA`. The `$TCA` field definitions are described in the **TYPO3 Core API** document. For example, the `templateFile` field is of type `input`. Looking at **TYPO3 Core API** for `input` fields will show properties such as `eval` or `default` and will explain their meaning. Thus, it is possible to create new flexform fields by referring to the **TYPO3 Core API**.

If a flexform has several sheets, the data source changes a little:

```
<T3DataStructure>
   <meta>
      <langDisable>1</langDisable>
   </meta>
   <sheets>
      <sDEF>
         <ROOT>
            <TCEforms>
               <sheetTitle>
                  LLL:EXT:irfaq/lang/locallang_db.xml:
                  tx_irfaq.pi_flexform.sheet_general</sheetTitle>
            </TCEforms>
            <type>array</type>
            <el>
```

```
                </el>
            </ROOT>
        </sDEF>
        <sCATEGORIES>
            <ROOT>
                <TCEforms>
                <sheetTitle>
                    LLL:EXT:irfaq/lang/locallang_db.xml:
                    tx_irfaq.pi_flexform.sheet_categories</sheetTitle>
                </TCEforms>
                <type>array</type>
                <el>

                </el>
            </ROOT>
        </sCATEGORIES>
        <sSEARCH>
            <ROOT>
                <TCEforms>
                    <sheetTitle>
                        LLL:EXT:irfaq/lang/locallang_db.xml:
                        tx_irfaq.pi_flexform.sheet_search</sheetTitle>
                </TCEforms>
                <type>array</type>
                <el>

                </el>
            </ROOT>
        </sSEARCH>
    </sheets>
</T3DataStructure>
```

In this case, field definitions are moved inside sheets. Sheets identifiers must start with the letter s and will preferably be in upper case. These identifiers will be used as the third parameter of the pi_getFFvalue() function. The sheetTitle tag defines the title for the sheet in the Backend.

To include the flexform in the plugin, the ext_tables.php file should be modified to include the following lines:

```
$TCA['tt_content']['types']['list']['subtypes_addlist']
        [$_EXTKEY . '_pi1'] = 'pi_flexform';
t3lib_extMgm::addPiFlexFormValue($_EXTKEY .  '_pi1',
        'FILE:EXT:' . $_EXTKEY . 'pi1/flexform_ds.xml');
```

Do not forget to clear the configuration cache in the Backend to apply these changes.

Templating

One feature of a successful website is its unique look. A website designer should be able to modify the website appearance according to the website's purpose. It means that the plugin output should be modifiable as well. This is achieved by making the plugin output using templates.

TYPO3 has built-in support for templates. A template is a normal HTML file where data and text strings are replaced with special **markers**. A marker usually looks like this: ###MARKER###. There are two types of markers:

- Plain marker (replaces the marker by data)
- Subsection marker (replaces everything between two markers by data)

Here is an example of a template:

```
<!DOCTYPE html PUBLIC
        "-//W3C//DTD HTML 4.01 Transitional//EN"
        "http://www.w3.org/TR/html4/loose.dtd">
<html>
<head>
<title>Sample template</title>
</head>
<body>
<h1>Results template</h1>
<!-- ###RESULTS### begin -->
<div class="tx_myext_results">
    ###TEXT_RESULTS###:
    <!-- ###RESULT_SUB### begin -->
        <br />
        ###FIELD_TITLE###: ###FIELD_VALUE###
    <!-- ###RESULT_SUB### end -->
</div>
<!-- ###RESULTS### end -->
</body>
</html>
```

Here, ###RESULTS### is a template for a part of the Frontend output. The plugin will extract it from the file and use it to format the output. ###TEXT_RESULTS### will be replaced with a simple label from the language file. The plugin will extract ###RESULT_SUB### as a subsection and use it repeatedly for each field to produce output.

Here is sample code that uses this template:

```
// Get template content
$templateCode = $this->cObj->fileResource(
        $this->conf['templateFile']);
// Extract part surrounded by ###RESULTS###
$resultsTemplate = $this->cObj->getSubpart($templateCode,
        '###RESULTS###');
// Extract part surrounded by ###RESULT_SUB###
$resultSub = $this->cObj->getSubpart($templateCode,
        '###RESULT_SUB###');
$fieldList = '';
// Loop through fields and create a list of them for Frontend
foreach ($fields as $title => $value) {
    $fieldList .= $this->cObj->substituteMarkerArray(
                $resultSub, array(
                    '###FIELD_TITLE###' =>
                        htmlspecialchars($title),
                    '###FIELD_VALUE###' =>
                        htmlspecialchars($value),
            ));
}
// Compile output
$output = $this->cObj->substituteMarkerArrayCached(
        $resultsTemplate, array(
            '###TEXT_RESULTS###' =>
                $this->pi_getLL('text_results'),
        ), array(
            '###RESULTS_SUB###' => $fieldList,
        ));
```

$this->cObj is an instance of the tslib_cObj class, which is created by TYPO3 for the plugin automatically.

It is possible to extract information using markers from any part of the file. For example, the following code adds data inside a page's <head> tag:

```
$subPart = $this->cObj->getSubpart($templateCode,
                '###HEADER_ADDITIONS###');
// Ensure that header part is added only once to the page
// even if plugin is inserted to the page more than once
$key = $this->prefixId . '_' . md5($subPart);
if (!isset($GLOBALS['TSFE']->additionalHeaderData[$key])) {
    $GLOBALS['TSFE']->additionalHeaderData[$key] =
        $this->cObj->substituteMarkerArray($subPart, array(
            '###SITE_REL_PATH###' =>
                t3lib_extMgm::siteRelPath($this->extKey),
        ));
}
```

The corresponding template would be:

```
<!DOCTYPE html PUBLIC
    "-//W3C//DTD HTML 4.01 Transitional//EN"
    "http://www.w3.org/TR/html4/loose.dtd">
<html>
<head>
<title>Sample template</title>
<!-- ###HEADER_ADDITIONS### begin -->
<link rel="stylesheet"
    href="###SITE_REL_PATH###res/pi1.css" />
<!-- ###HEADER_ADDITIONS### end -->
</head>
<body>
```

This will include the corresponding header additions when the plugin is included on the page. A website designer will be able to provide a template using a plugin configuration and customize the template according to the website's needs.

Localization

Localization is one of the important topics in TYPO3. TYPO3 is being used all over the world and users prefer to see it in their own language. The same applies to extensions. This section covers issues related to localization.

Being Localization-Aware

Different countries use different formats for numbers and dates. While TYPO3 includes configuration parameters for date and time, it is better to make such parameters configurable in an extension. It is preferable to use sprintf() for formatting numbers. Formatting dates is more complex because there are two choices: the date() and the strftime() functions. Localization-aware plugins should use the strftime() function because it has much better localization support than the date() function. In particular, it can show months and days according to the current language and locale.

Localizing Strings

A plugin should not have hard-coded strings. All strings should be in the locallang. xml file. This ensures that the plugin can be translated into other languages.

One important issue with localized strings is how such strings should be placed into the file. For example, consider the following string on a website:

```
Page 1 of 10
```

The wrong approach would be to create this code:

```
$content = $this->pi_getLL('page') .
              $currentPage .
              $this->pi_getLL('of') .
              $totalPages;
```

This code works fine with English, but most likely, it will not be usable with other languages. Other languages may have a different word order or even different ways of showing page information. The right way would be to create a string in `locallang.xml` that looks like this:

```
Page %1$d of %2$d
```

Note that the string not only has format specifiers but also positions of arguments. These can also change in other languages.

Corresponding PHP code is:

```
$content = sprintf($this->pi_getLL('page_info'),
                $currentPage, $totalPages);
```

It is even shorter and more readable.

Another important issue is which characters are allowed as string identifiers.

Kickstarter generates identifiers with a dot in them. Such identifiers work fine in the Backend, but they should not be used in the Frontend. A string from `locallang.xml` can be overridden using TypoScript, where the dot is a reserved character. Therefore, do not use a dot in string identifiers that will be used in the Frontend. Use the underscore character instead.

Fetching Localized Records

Sometimes, records contain language dependent data as well. Kickstarter is able to generate tables so that they will contain overlaid records. In this case, records should be obtained from the database using an additional SQL condition (`sys_language_uid=0`).

After fetching, the record in the default language should be overlaid with a language record. Here is the code:

```
$overlaidRow = $GLOBALS['TSFE']->sys_page->getRecordOverlay(
            $table, $row, $language,
            $GLOBALS['TSFE']->config['config']
            ['sys_language_overlay']);
```

The behavior of the function depends on the system configuration for translation. The **CONFIG** section TSRef document describes possible localization settings in more detail. The reader may be also interested in the **Frontend localization guide** document, which fully documents all aspects of localization handling in TYPO3. The whole topic is again too large to discuss in this book.

The $row variable passed to the function must contain the full record from the table (that is, selected with * as the field list). Note that the returned result may be empty if there is no record in the specified language. $language is a numeric language ID from the sys_languages table.

Character Set Handling

TYPO3 is able to work with different character sets. Frontend plugins must produce output in the proper character set. If all strings come from locallang.xml, it is usually not a problem. Therefore, strings should not be hard-coded in templates, but should come from the language file. It is a good habit to use ###**TEXT**_SOMETHING### for static strings.

TYPO3 has several different character set settings that affect the Frontend. They are listed in the following table:

Character set variable	Description
$TYPO3_CONF_VARS['BE']['forceCharset']	The character set for the Backend. All data entered in Backend is stored in the database using this character set.
$GLOBALS['TSFE']->defaultCharSet	The default character set for the Frontend output. Used only if none of the other variables is set.
$GLOBALS['TSFE']->renderCharset	The character set used to render the Frontend output. Usually, identical to the Backend character set to avoid character set conversions. Many extensions will not work properly if their value is different from the Backend character set.
$GLOBALS['TSFE']->metaCharset	The character set of the page as seen by a user. TYPO3 automatically converts a page from renderCharset to metaCharset after rendering.

While TYPO3 tries to make the character set processing transparent for plugins, there is at least one case when a plugin should be aware of the character sets.

If a plugin shows formatted data from the database, it may need to shorten strings. The normal PHP substr() function does not work with all character sets. TYPO3 has its own class to "fix" PHP 's shortcomings when proper character handling is necessary.

The following code shows how to crop lines in the Frontend plugins properly:

```
$GLOBALS['TSFE']->csConvObj->crop(
        $GLOBALS['TSFE']->renderCharset, $string,
        $numberOfChars, '...');
```

This code crops $string to a number of characters identified by $numberOfChars and appends three dots after the string. It uses renderCharset to be compatible with the rest of the Frontend rendering.

Caching

Caching is an extremely important topic in TYPO3. If an extension does not work properly with cache, it may slow down pages significantly. Therefore, cache related issues should always be considered by extension developers while developing Frontend plugins.

Caching in TYPO3

TYPO3 caches all pages by default. Caching means that the page content is generated once and stored to the database. When a user visits the same page again, TYPO3 does not have to generate all the menus, process all the content objects, or call the Frontend plugins once again. It simply takes the page content from the database and sends it to the website visitor. Caching is able to speed up page rendering about 10-20 times.

While caching, TYPO3 must take care of many issues. For example, a page can be available in many languages. There can be Frontend users logged in. A page may have parameters such as the news article ID. All these issues affect caching.

A page can be cached either to the database or to the external files. TYPO3 decides it using configuration value, which is the same for every site in the current installation. How pages are cached makes no difference to plugins.

If pages are not cached, this will seriously affect the performance of TYPO3 websites. Extensions must not prevent whole page caching under any condition.

Cached and Non-Cached Output

What happens if a developer needs to create a plugin that must produce different output at each page reload? It means that the code must be executed every time the page is shown to a user. How this can be achieved without preventing page cache?

TYPO3 makes it possible for extensions to produce noncacheable output. In this case, TYPO3 creates normal cacheable content for the rest of the page but does not execute noncached plugins. Instead, TYPO3 inserts special markers to the cached output. Each time the page is fetched from the cache, TYPO3 instantiates a plugin and executes its code. So, the page gets dynamically generated content all the time.

While the idea sounds attractive, noncached plugins should be used only when necessary. They still affect performance.

How does TYPO3 determine whether a plugin should be cached or not? Typically, a plugin is either a USER or a USER_INT object. The first one is cached, while the second is not.

Noncached plugins have certain limitations. They are executed when the rest of the page is already generated. So, noncached plugins cannot add data inside the `<head>` tag, cannot change page title and cannot transfer data to noncached plugins. They also do not have access to fully parsed TypoScript setup inside $TSFE. But these limitations are usually not too important.

Yet another small, but important difference between cached and noncached plugins is their configuration. Since TYPO3 does not have parsed TypoScript setup when executing noncached plugins, it must know how to load a noncached plugin. Typically, a cached plugin is configured like this:

```
plugin.tx_myext_pi1 = USER
plugin.tx_myext_pi1 {
   userFunc = tx_myext_pi1->main
}
```

Whereas noncached plugins are configured like this:

```
plugin.tx_myext_pi1 = USER
plugin.tx_myext_pi1 {
   includeLibs = EXT:myext/pi1/class.tx_myext_pi1.php
   userFunc = tx_myext_pi1->main
}
```

The line in bold tells TYPO3 where `userFunc` is located. If this line is missing, the noncached plugin will not be loaded and will not produce any output. In other words, it will be silently ignored by TYPO3.

Using cHash

What happens if extension output is based on the parameters? For example, the news system must accept the news item ID and generate content based on this ID. Obviously, if a page is cached for one ID, it will be just returned from the cache for another ID.

One solution would be to create a noncached plugin. This is how such tasks were solved in the past by many plugins. However, there is a better solution.

TYPO3 allows us to cache pages using page parameters. This is made possible through cHash, which stands for content hash.

cHash is a checksum of the page parameters. When TYPO3 sees cHash in the list of parameters, it takes all other parameters and computes the checksum. If the checksum matches, it fetches the cached content that matches the page ID and the cHash value. When the news article ID changes, cHash will change as well, and TYPO3 will fetch a proper cached version of the page.

Can cHash be faked? It cannot unless the attacker can view the content of the typo3conf/localconf.php file. This file contains the value of the security key that is used in cHash computation.

How can a developer create code that uses cHash? This can be done either directly by using the typoLink function of tslib_cObj, or by using the pi_link family of functions from the tslib_pibase class. Here is a code example showing the use of typoLink:

```
$conf = array(
    'parameter' => $GLOBALS['TSFE']->id,
    'useCacheHash' => true,
    'additionalParams' => '&tx_myext_pi1[param]=123',
);
$linkedText = $this->cObj->typoLink('my link', $conf);
$link = $this->cObj->lastTypoLinkUrl;
```

When using the pi_link functions, an extension must ensure that $pi_USER_INT_obj is set to false and $pi_cacheCHash is set to true. Here is a code example:

```
$text = $this->pi_linkTP('my link text', array(
            'tx_myext[param]' => 123,
        ), true);
```

This generates linked text. There are other functions in tslib_pibase that create just a link or allow us to reuse and override some URL parameters. They are useful in many cases, but the typoLink example is the most universal. All tslib_pibase functions are just wrapped around typoLink.

Two Things to Avoid

When it comes to caching while developing Frontend plugins, there are two things to be avoided at all costs:

no_cache=1

This URL parameter is often improperly used when an extension submits some information to itself. A page is not cached and the USER plugin executes and processes submission. While it prevents page caching, it does so only when a submission happens, so it does not look too bad. But it should be avoided. For such cases, a page should contain the USER_INT plugin. Even if it does not produce any output, it can still process submissions and generate error messages.

set_no_cache()

There is a function in $TSFE that can be used to prevent caching. That function should never ever be used from extensions.

Advanced: Embedding USER_INT into USER

If an extension already uses no_cache=1 or set_no_cache() and it cannot be split into cached and noncached plugins due to compatibility reasons, it is still possible to make a proper plugin. The idea behind this technique is to embed the USER_INT plugin inside the USER plugin. Technically, it is done in the following way:

```
$content = 'My USER plugin content';
$cObj = t3lib_div::makeInstance('tslib_cObj');
/* @var $cObj tslib_cObj */
$cObj->start(array());
$conf = $GLOBALS['TSFE']->tmpl->setup
            ['plugin.']['tx_myext_pi2.'];
$conf['includeLibs'] =
    'EXT:myext/pi2/class.tx_myext_pi2.php';
$content .= $cObj->cObjGetSingle('USER_INT', $conf);
$content .= 'Rest of my USER plugin content';
```

The code fragment given here produces noncached content inside cached content. Using this technique, it is easy to convert existing extensions from using no_cache=1 to using noncached plugins.

Summary

In this chapter, we looked into the details of the Frontend plugin programming. In the next chapter, we will use these techniques to create a Frontend plugin.

It must be noted here that Frontend plugins are usually not made in the form of a single function. Normally, they are classes, and typically extend a class named `tslib_pibase`. Having a class allows us to implement complex logic using many functions and to keep working on data as class attributes. The example above should be really treated as an example, not as a recommendation on creating plugins. A proper plugin must be a class!

6
Programming Frontend Plugins

In this chapter, we will learn more about Frontend plugins and create our own plugin. We will learn best practices and certain tricks that come handy when creating really good plugins. We will also review and become familiar with **eID**–one of the most mysterious parts of TYPO3.

There will be a lot of code fragments in this chapter (but not complete files). In this book, these fragments are formatted for better presentation. The real code may be formatted differently. The reader is encouraged to get a copy of the code from Packt Publishing's website and look into the actual files while reading.

Some extra functionality is left for the reader to finish or implement better. Since we will only learn plugin coding, our purpose in this chapter is to show how to do it properly. Often nice features are simplified to give more space for implementation details.

Review and Update Generated Files

Kickstarer generated several Frontend plugin files for us and added several code lines to ensure proper configuration of the plugin. Let's see what exactly was generated and how it is related to the plugin. We will also adjust certain lines to better fit our needs.

Frontend Plugin Files

Frontend plugin files are located in the `pi1` directory of our extension. Kickstarter generated two files: `class.tx_feuserlist_pi1.php` and `locallang.xml`. The first file contains the plugin code, while the second contains language strings for the plugin.

class.tx_feuserlist_pi1.php

This is the file that TYPO3 will include as part of the Frontend plugin execution process. As we already know from the previous chapters, according to TYPO3 coding guidelines, the file will contain the `tx_feuserlist_pi1` PHP class.

Each class file starts with GPL license. It must appear in every TYPO3 related code file. Next goes a special comment, which looks like this:

```
/**
 * [CLASS/FUNCTION INDEX of SCRIPT]
 *
 * Hint: use extdeveval to insert/update function index above.
 */
```

The `extdeveval` extension can generate a listing of all functions inside the file. An example of such a listing can be seen in the core files. It shows the function name, parameters, and the line number. It would be useful to quickly look up the parameters of the function. While generating such listings, `extdeveval` will look for the marker from the second line in the code above. Often programmers add Subversion or CVS markers (such as `$Id$`) to this part of the file.

Next goes the `require_once` PHP call to include the `tslib_pibase` class – the base class of the plugin class.

Next, Kickstarter generates the plugin class prefixed by a PHPDoc comment. The class contains four class attributes (variables):

Name	Type	Description
`$prefixId`	string	This is a prefix for plugin parameters in URLs. This variable is required by `tslib_pibase` and its use is highly recommended in the code because it simplifies code copying and reusing in other plugins.
		By default, the value of this attribute is equal to the plugin class name.
`$scriptRelPath`	string	This is a relative path to the plugin's PHP file (the file where this class is located). It is also used by `tslib_pibase`.
`$extKey`	string	Extension key; also used by `tslib_pibase`.
`$pi_checkCHash`	boolean	This attribute is described in the previous chapter. It is used for caching pages whose content depends on the URL parameters. It is created and set to `true` by default for all USER (cached) plugins.

Variables are followed by the `main()` function. This function is defined in the TypoScript setup as the entry point of the plugin. The function accepts two parameters:

Name	Type	Value
$content	string	Normally empty but can be set if the plugin is called by another plugin
$conf	array	TypoScript configuration array. For example, consider the following TypoScript:

```
plugin.tx_mext_pi1 = USER
plugin.tx_myext_pi1 {
   userFunc = tx_myext_pi1->main
   param1 = value1
   param1 {
      param2 = value2
   }
}
```

Plugin will receive this TypoScript as follows:

```
$conf = array(
  'userFunc' =>
            'tx_myext_pi1->main',
  'param1' => 'value1',
  'param1.' => array(
     'param2' => 'value2',
  ),
);
```

Notice how `param1` is passed as a value first and then as an array by using a dot.

The generated function contains a sample implementation. The first three lines are usually kept in every implementation:

```
$this->conf = $conf;
$this->pi_setPiVarDefaults();
$this->pi_loadLL();
```

The first line must always be present in the plugin and must be one of the first lines executed by the plugin. `tslib_pibase` (plugin's base class) depends on this value.

The next line calls a function that checks the TypoScript setup for the `_DEFAULT_PI_VARS` array property and sets the values of `$this->piVars` from this array, if it is set. Normally, `$this->piVars` contains parameters passed to the plugin in the URL (in the form of `tx_extkey_pi1[param]=value`). This function can provide defaults if the parameter is not set in the URL. We will see it later in this chapter.

The last line loads translated strings from the `locallang.xml` file. It allows the use of the `$this->pi_getLL()` function to obtain such strings. This is necessary because the `$LANG` object is not available in the Frontend by default. Additionally, this function checks if translations are overlaid from the TypoScript by using the `_LOCAL_LANG` array property.

The rest of the code contains sample plugin output, which we will replace during development.

locallang.xml

This is an XML file with translated strings. By default, it contains sample strings. The file uses UTF-8 encoding and looks like this:

```
<?xml version="1.0" encoding="utf-8" standalone="yes" ?>
<T3locallang>
    <meta type="array">
        <type>module</type>
        <description>Language labels for plugin &quot;tx_feuserstat_
pi1&quot;</description>
    </meta>
    <data type="array">
        <languageKey index="default" type="array">
            <label index="list_mode_1">Mode 1</label>
            <label index="list_mode_2">Mode 2</label>
            <label index="list_mode_3">Mode 3</label>
            <label index="back">Back</label>
            <label index="submit_button_label">Click here to submit
value</label>
        </languageKey>
    </data>
</T3locallang>
```

Strings are added inside `languageKey` as `label` entries. The `index` attribute of `languageKey` tells which language is used for this section. The term `default` implies English, while other languages typically use codes such as `de` for German or `fr` for French. Do not put labels in your native language into the `default` section. This violates TYPO3 conventions. They must be in English!

During development, an extension may have strings for various languages inside `locallang.xml`. This is also true for private (non-public) extensions. However, if an extension is distributed publicly, all labels (except for the default language) should be extracted to language packs and distributed through the translation service of TYPO3 Extension Manager. To extract labels, an extension should be installed on the translation server. Then an extension can also be translated into other languages. More information about translation is available in TYPO3 wiki at `http://wiki.typo3.org/`.

Other Related Files

Other files are located outside the plugin directory, but they also participate in the Frontend plugin work and should therefore be observed. They seriously affect the plugin's work.

TypoScript Files

TypoScript files are placed inside the `static` directory in the extension. Kickstarter generates only one subdirectory inside the `static` directory, which is derived from the TypoScript template name entered in the corresponding Kickstarter step. Developers can add other subdirectories, but they must also register new templates in the `ext_tables.php` file as shown in the following `ext_tables.php` description.

Kickstarter generated the `frontend_user_list` subdirectory for our extension. This file contains `constants.txt` and `setup.txt` with the text that we entered during extension generation.

ext_localconf.php

This file is very short:

```php
<?php
if (!defined ('TYPO3_MODE')) {
    die ('Access denied.');
}
t3lib_extMgm::addPItoST43($_EXTKEY,
        'pi1/class.tx_feuserstat_pi1.php', '_pi1',
        'list_type', 1);
?>
```

The first three lines prevent direct file execution from the browser window if someone types the URL of the file in the browser window.

The remaining code creates default TypoScript for the plugin. Strictly speaking, it is not necessary, but it allows your extension to be called (and report configuration errors) even if the extension's TypoScript code is not included in the main TypoScript template of the web site. We will use this functionality in our plugin.

ext_tables.php

The abridged version of ext_tables.php is shown here:

```php
<?php
if (!defined ('TYPO3_MODE')) {
    die ('Access denied.');
}

t3lib_extMgm::addStaticFile($_EXTKEY,
        'static/frontend_user_list/', 'Frontend user list');
t3lib_div::loadTCA('tt_content');
$TCA['tt_content']['types']['list']['subtypes_excludelist']
        [$_EXTKEY.'_pi1'] = 'layout,select_key';
t3lib_extMgm::addPlugin(array(
'LLL:EXT:feuserstat/locallang_db.xml:tt_content.list_type_pi1'
, $_EXTKEY . '_pi1'), 'list_type');
?>
```

The call to t3lib_extMgm::addStaticFile() registers the extension's TypoScript code with TYPO3. Now, the "Frontend user list" will be available in the "Include static (from extensions)" while editing the TypoScript setup. It should be added to the main TypoScript template for proper functioning of the plugin.

The next two lines modify the web form look of the plugin. Firstly, the table configuration array is loaded for the tt_content table. Next, two old fields are excluded from the list of displayed fields. Modern extensions do not use these fields, so Kickstarter generates this code automatically.

The remaining code adds the plugin into the list of plugins in the web form for content elements. This list is seen when a user uses "Insert plugin" type for content element items.

Non-Reviewed Files

There are some other files that were generated but not reviewed so far. They contain functionality for our Backend module and will be reviewed in detail in the next chapter.

Clean Up Extension

Before we proceed to programming, we need to make certain adjustments to the generated extension and add new files and directories.

At the time of writing this book, the Kickstarter extension did not fully follow TYPO3 coding guidelines. Therefore, the extension has to be adjusted to follow these guidelines closer. This may not be the fact when the reader reads this book because Kickstater could already be fixed. Nevertheless, we will see what needs to be changed in the generated code.

Here is a list of nonconforming items produced by Kickstarter:

- Using double quotes instead of single
- Missing spaces around the string concatenation operator (dot)
- Missing spaces after commas
- Lines longer than 80 characters

While these items do not affect functionality, they should be cleaned up because code must use consistent coding style.

Programming the Plugin

In this section, we will create our plugin and related code.

General Workflow

We will follow the top-down principle in development. We will start with big blocks and then go into details. We will use small functions that call other small functions to perform isolated functions. This creates cleaner applications that are much easier to debug, and it is much faster to fix or re-implement any functionality, if necessary.

Adding Files

Before we proceed with implementation, we need to create several additional files. We will use these files later during implementation. Generally, if a feature is used, it is better to have a skeleton of such files created in the very beginning. Later, information can be simply added there when necessary. There will be no need to be distracted from the main development course to create these files from scratch.

Templates

We will use templates in the Frontend plugins. Designers will be able to either customize the default template or create a new one based on the default.

First, we create a directory named `res` in the root directory of the extension. Next, we create three files there:

- `pi1_template.html`
- `pi1.css`
- `pi1.js`

The last two files will be empty for now. The first file is the simplest HTML file possible:

```
<html>
<head>
<title>pi1 plugin template file</title>
</head>
<body>
</body>
</html>
```

We will add template data to this file later.

Flexform Configuration

Modern templates have two means of configuration: TypoScript configuration and Flexform configuration. The first one can be seen as base configuration. It can be used when a plugin is inserted into a page through TypoScript, or when it is inserted using the **Page** module. Flexform configuration is limited to plugins inserted as records to the page (usually using the **Page** module).

Though TypoScript configuration is enough in most cases, users may feel more comfortable if a plugin provides configuration also through flexforms.

Flexform configuration is stored in an XML format **data source** or DS, for short. We will create the smallest file and add entries there when we program the plugin. Here is the file:

```
<?xml version="1.0" encoding="UTF-8"?>
<T3DataStructure>
   <meta>
      <langDisable>1</langDisable>
      <langChildren>0</langChildren>
   </meta>
   <ROOT>
      <type>array</type>
      <el>
      </el>
   </ROOT>
</T3DataStructure>
```

This file should be placed in `pi1/flexform_ds.xml`.

eID

The eID is TYPO3's way of quickly providing response to certain types of queries without invoking the whole TYPO3 Frontend. It is used by the TYPO3 enlarge-on-click feature, which is useful, for example, in the AJAX applications. Since this feature is very powerful but lacks documentation, we will use it in our extension for learning purposes. The same task can be performed without eID, but our main purpose is to learn extension programming.

The eID file is a normal PHP class named `tx_feuserstat_eID`. We will place it inside the extension's directory and name it `class.tx_feuserstat_eid.php`. The content of the file is not shown here due to its size. But it is a typical TYPO3 class with GPL at the top and XCLASS declaration at the bottom. You will find it in the code companion supplied with this book.

In addition to the class, we need to register it in `ext_localconf.php`:

```
// eID
$GLOBALS['TYPO3_CONF_VARS']['FE']['eID_include']
    ['feuserstat'] =
        'EXT:feuserstat/class.tx_feuserstat_eid.php';
```

Do not forget to clear the configuration cache after adding these lines to make them effective.

Defining Functions

Our plugin will logically consist of several areas:

- Initialization, which includes the following:
  - Checking for correct environment
  - Loading configuration
- Single view for `fe_user` records
- Paged list view
- Search

The search function will call eID to load data for a Google-like autocomplete feature. While it is not strictly necessary, it is a good way to show how eID works. The search form itself will be a part of the list view.

Since logical areas are identified, we can create empty functions in the class inside
`pi1/class.tx_feuserstat_pi1.php`:

```
/**
 * Initializes plugin configuration.
 *
 * @return      string Generated HTML
 */
protected function init() {
}
/**
 * Shows single user card.
 *
 * @return      string Generated HTML
 */
protected function singleView() {
   return '';
}
/**
 * Shows user list.
 *
 * @return      string Generated HTML
 */
protected function listView() {
   return '';
}
```

Here, we use PHP5 features, making methods protected to prevent uncontrolled calls
from outside the class and type hinting for function parameters whenever possible
according to PHP syntax. While it may seem to be useless to use type hinting in a
protected function, it is a good habit to use type hinting anywhere. If using code
hinting becomes automatic to a developer, it may prevent many strange errors later.

Now, after we build a skeleton for development, we start development! We will start
with the first logical thing: initialization of the extension.

Initializing an Extension

Initialization of an extension consists of two parts:

- Checking the environment and making sure that the extension can work.
- Preparing parameters and setting defaults if parameters are not set explicitly.

These two tasks are usually the first that a plugin does.

Checking the Environment

Checking the environment ensures that an extension can work properly. Typically, an extension requires some options to be set. Defaults are normally set through TypoScript. However, it is easy to forget to include the TypoScript template from an extension to the main website template. In this case, all default options will not be available. This is to be checked during initialization.

The other things to be checked depend on the extension's logic. It may be page availability to the current user or in the current context, Frontend user status (logged in or not) or anything else that you can think of. The more checks a plugin contains, the fewer are the chances of unseen errors and instability.

We start with checking whether the TypoScript template for our plugin has been included in the main template of the site. We check whether usersPid is set in the $conf parameter. If not, we return an error message (here and later added or modified code lines are in **bold**):

```
public function main($content, $conf) {
    $this->conf = $conf;
    $this->pi_setPiVarDefaults();
    $this->pi_loadLL();
    // Check environment
    if (!isset($conf['usersPid'])) {
        return $this->pi_wrapInBaseClass(

            $this->pi_getLL('no_ts_template'));
    }
    $content = '';
    return $this->pi_wrapInBaseClass($content);
}
```

While this check may seem insignificant, it really does work. It is amazing how many people forget to add plugin's TypoScript template to the website template. They will thank you for the provided hint.

To show an error message, we also add the corresponding string to pi1/ locallang.xml.

Other TypoScript parameters may be empty, but we can substitute good defaults for them.

Loading Configuration

The next step in development is to load configuration values. Since we are going to use two ways of configuration (TypoScript and Flexform), we need to merge values. For that, we will create a new function:

```
/**
 * Fetches configuration value given its name.
 * Merges flexform and TS configuration values.
 *
 * @param     string $param Configuration value name
 * @return    string Parameter value
 */
protected function fetchConfigurationValue($param) {
    $value = trim($this->pi_getFFvalue(
        $this->cObj->data['pi_flexform'], $param));
    return $value ? $value : $this->conf[$param];
}
```

The `$this->cObj->data` function contains the `tt_content` record, which is a record of our plugin. When the Backend user saves the configuration, flexform is converted to XML and saved to the database field named `pi_flexform`. The `pi_getFFvalue` function extracts a value from a flexform array. The XML inside the `pi_flexform` database field is transformed into an array by calling the `pi_initPIflexform` function, which will be the first thing to do in the plugin's `init` function.

The `fetchConfigurationValue` function returns a value from flexform if it is set. Otherwise, it returns a value from TypoScript.

Next, we have the `init` function working:

```
protected function init() {
    $this->pi_initPIflexForm();
    // Get values
    $this->conf['usersPid'] =
        intval($this->fetchConfigurationValue('usersPid'));
    $this->conf['singlePid'] =
        intval($this->fetchConfigurationValue('singlePid'));
    $this->conf['listPid'] =
        intval($this->fetchConfigurationValue('listPid'));
    $this->conf['templateFile'] =
        $this->fetchConfigurationValue('templateFile');
    // Set defaults if necessary
    if (!$this->conf['usersPid']) {
        $GLOBALS['TT']->setTSlogMessage(
                'Warning: usersPid is not set in ' .
```

```
            $this->prefixId .
            ' plugin. No users will be shown!', 2);
    }
    if (!$this->conf['singlePid']) {
        $this->conf['singlePid'] = $GLOBALS['TSFE']->id;
    }
    if (!$this->conf['listPid']) {
        $this->conf['listPid'] = $GLOBALS['TSFE']->id;
    }
    if (!$this->conf['templateFile']) {
        $this->conf['templateFile'] =
            'EXT:' . $this->extKey . '/res/pi1_template.html';
    }
    // Load template code
    $this->templateCode =
        $this->cObj->fileResource(
            $this->conf['templateFile']);
}
```

Firstly, the function initializes flexform. Next, it fetches all the parameters converting all the page `uid` values to integers. Doing it once allows us to use these values in SQL queries without additional `intval` calls.

Next, the function sets default values if real values are not provided. We only skip `usersPid` here because we cannot give any reasonable default. But we set the logging message to the admin panel to show the warning about it. Note that we do not hard-code the plugin name but use `$this->prefixId`. The code is not plugin-dependent anymore. Using `$this->prefixId` helps to copy/paste such code into other extensions when necessary.

The last part loads the HTML file into a class attribute. The `$this->cObj->fileResource` function understands several ways to specify the path to a file (including `EXT:` syntax) and returns the file content for most files (for image files, this function returns `<img>` tag).

The last thing we must do to finish initialization is to add a call to `init` into the `main` function.

Modifying the Flexform Data Source

Now, we need to modify the flexform data source file to add new fields there. While adding fields, a developer should refer to the **TYPO3 Core API** document, which is available at `http://typo3.org/`. The syntax of flexform DS roughly corresponds to the syntax of `$TCA` field definitions.

We add four fields to the data source. They correspond to the fields in the plugin's TypoScript setup. Fields will have the same names as the TypoScript values to be compatible with the plugin initialization functions. Fields are added between `<el>` and `</el>` XML tags.

The first field is `usersPid`:

```
<usersPid>
    <TCEforms>
        <label>LLL:EXT:feuserstat/locallang_db.xml:
pi1_flexform.usersPid</label>
        <config>
            <type>group</type>
            <internal_type>db</internal_type>
            <allowed>pages</allowed>
            <prepend_tname>0</prepend_tname>
            <minitems>0</minitems>
            <maxitems>1</maxitems>
            <size>1</size>
        </config>
    </TCEforms>
</usersPid>
```

Looking at **TYPO3 Core API** reveals the following:

- The label is stored in the language file named `locallang_db.xml` in the extension's directory.
- The field's type is `group`.
- The field contains a single (`maxitems` is 1) reference to the `pages` table.
- The control will be one line high.

The next two fields are `singlePid` and `listPid`. They are almost identical to `usersPid` (except for the label):

```
<singlePid>
    <TCEforms>
        <label>LLL:EXT:feuserstat/locallang_db.xml:
pi1_flexform.singlePid</label>
        <config>
            <type>group</type>
            <internal_type>db</internal_type>
            <allowed>pages</allowed>
            <prepend_tname>0</prepend_tname>
            <minitems>0</minitems>
            <maxitems>1</maxitems>
```

```
            <size>1</size>
        </config>
    </TCEforms>
</singlePid>
<listPid>
    <TCEforms>
        <label>LLL:EXT:feuserstat/locallang_db.xml:
pi1_flexform.listPid</label>
        <config>
            <type>group</type>
            <internal_type>db</internal_type>
            <allowed>pages</allowed>
            <prepend_tname>0</prepend_tname>
            <minitems>0</minitems>
            <maxitems>1</maxitems>
            <size>1</size>
        </config>
    </TCEforms>
</listPid>
```

The last field is the templateFile:

```
<templateFile>
    <TCEforms>
        <label>LLL:EXT:feuserstat/locallang_db.xml:
pi1_flexform.templateFile</label>
        <config>
            <type>input</type>
            <eval>trim</eval>
            <wizards type="array">
                <_PADDING>2</_PADDING>
                <link type="array">
                    <type>popup</type>
                    <title>Link</title>
                    <icon>link_popup.gif</icon>
                    <script>browse_links.php?
mode=wizard&amp;act=file</script>
                    <params type="array">
                        <blindLinkOptions>page,url,mail,spec
</blindLinkOptions>
                    </params>
                    <JSopenParams>height=300,width=500,
status=0,menubar=0,scrollbars=1</JSopenParams>
```

```
        </link>
      </wizards>
    </config>
  </TCEforms>
</templateFile>
```

Note how the **Template file** field is created in the flexform. Traditionally, TYPO3 used upload fields for the template file. While this still can be used, it is not flexible enough. Typically, it is easier for a website designer or website owner to place the template file in the subdirectory of the `fileadmin/` directory. If the file is updated, it can be uploaded directly to the folder without changing the plugin instances on several pages.

The field has a wizard icon to the right of the input field. The wizard is a standard TYPO3 window where a file can be selected. All irrelevant options are hidden by the wizard configuration.

The only remaining task now is to tell TYPO3 to use the flexform. We do it in `ext_tables.php`:

```
$TCA['tt_content']['types']['list']['subtypes_excludelist']
      [$_EXTKEY . '_pi1'] = 'layout,select_key,pages';
$TCA['tt_content']['types']['list']['subtypes_addlist']
      [$_EXTKEY . '_pi1'] = 'pi_flexform';
t3lib_extMgm::addPiFlexFormValue($_EXTKEY . '_pi1',
      'FILE:EXT:' . $_EXTKEY . '/pi1/flexform_ds.xml');
```

Here is what the flexform configuration looks like in the Backend:

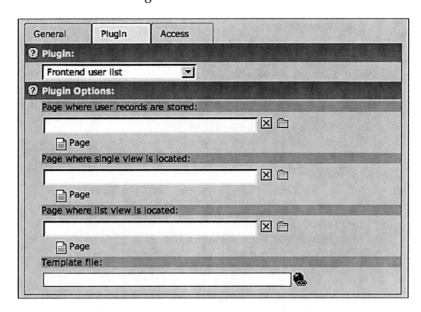

Dispatching Calls

Now, after we finished initialization, we will create dispatching code to direct control flow to the appropriate function according to the current plugin mode. This is very simple:

```
public function main($content, $conf) {
    $this->conf = $conf;
    $this->pi_setPiVarDefaults();
    $this->pi_loadLL();
    // Check environment
    if (!isset($conf['usersPid'])) {
        return $this->pi_wrapInBaseClass(
            $this->pi_getLL('no_ts_template'));
    }
    // Init
    $this->init();
    if (t3lib_div::testInt($this->piVars['showUid'])) {
        $content = $this->singleView();
    }
    else {
        $content = $this->listView();
    }
    return $this->pi_wrapInBaseClass($content);
}
```

We use `t3lib_div::testInt`, which returns `true` if and only if a parameter is a valid integer. The `showUid` function is traditionally used to pass the `uid` value of the single item to be shown.

Now, we are ready to proceed to the implementation of single and list views. But first we need to talk about using templates in a single view and a list view.

Using Templates

In this section, we will discuss how to use templates to provide customizable output for the website.

Template Basics

Templates make your plugins customizable. Anyone can provide his or her unique look to your plugin. This offers great flexibility to website creators, who can truly use the plugin in the context of the website.

A plugin template is usually a regular HTML file (though you can have text templates for mail or XML templates for RSS). Template files contain special tokens called markers. These markers are usually words in upper-case surrounded by three hash marks (###).

There are two types of markers:

- Plain markers
- Subsection markers

Here is an example:

```
<!-- ###LIST### begin -->
    ###CONTENT###
<!-- ###LIST### end -->
```

###LIST### is a subsection marker. ###CONTENT### is a plain marker. Plain markers are replaced with a single string. Subsection markers are trickier. They are also replaced as a whole and can be used for many purposes, for example:

- To repeat subsection content many times (for example, news items).
- To remove subsection content completely if necessary (for example, error subsection if there are no errors).
- To mark the beginning and the end of a subsection for the view (for example, one subsection for List and another for Single view).

How do we identify subsection markers? Firstly, they are usually placed inside comments. This is not truly an identifying sign because nothing prevents a template designer from commenting a plain marker. But a subsection marker always has a pair. And often a marker is followed by the begin and end keywords. These keywords are not mandatory. TYPO3 does not use them at all, but they help to locate the beginning and end of the section. Additionally, TYPO3 is smart enough to ignore anything else inside the comment tag. For example:

```
<!-- ###LIST### begin
    This is the template for the LIST view. It can contain the
    following markers:
      CONTENT   Marks content
  -->
    ###CONTENT###
<!-- ###LIST### end -->
```

Just make sure that you do not put another marker to the comment (that is, do not surround a marker name with hashes).

Using Templates

We have already seen functions that use templates in the previous chapters. They belong to the `tslib_cObj` class. The general workflow is as follows:

1. Obtain a subpart of the current plugin mode using `$this->cObj->getSubpart`.

2. Create an array with markers, where keys are markers and values are data values.

3. For each subpart, fetch the subpart, perform steps 1 and 2 for the subpart (in the loop, if necessary), and save output in a separate array.

4. Pass all data to `$this->cObj->substituteMarkerArrayCached`.

Let's see the code example. We will use the following template:

```
<html>
<head>
<title>Test</title>
</head>
<body>
<!-- ###LIST### begin -->
   ###TEXT_ITEMS###:
   <ul>
   <!-- ###ITEM### begin -->
      <li>###TEXT###</li>
   <!-- ###ITEM### end -->
   </ul>
<!-- ###LIST### end -->
</body>
</html>
```

The following code processes this template:

```
// Get main template
$template = $this->cObj->getSubpart($this->templateCode,
              '###LIST###');
// Create marker array
$markers = array(
    '###TEXT_ITEMS###' => $this->pi_getLL('items_in_the_list'),
);
// Get template for the subpart
$subTemplate = $this->cObj->getSubpart($template,
              '###ITEM###');
// Create item list
$itemList = '';
for ($i = 1; $i < 10; $i++) {
```

```
    $itemList = $this->substitureMarker($subTemplate,
                '###TEXT###', $i);
}
// Create array for subpart markers
$subMarkers = array(
    '###ITEM###' => $itemList,
);
// Create full output
return $this->cObj->substituteMarkerArrayCached(
            $this->template, $markers, $subMarkers);
```

The reader should be aware that substituteMarkerArrayCached caches the data into the cache_hash database table. This may be undesirable for plugins that call this function frequently and pass different data to it each time. Calling this function may create a lot of unused records in the database. The alternative is to call substituteSubpart in a loop.

Now that we know how to use templates, we proceed to look at creating a single view.

Creating a Single view

Creating a single view is simpler than creating a list view. We will assume that a single view can display almost every column (except password or other columns that make no sense to be displayed).

Creating a Template

To simplify template structure, we will create a table-based design for a template. In real life, you probably should use a CSS-based layout.

A template should be easily adjustable if new fields are added. Preferably, no code changes are required if the fe_users table is changed. For that, we will use markers such as ###TEXT_NAME### and ###FIELD_NAME###. Any new field can be added to a template in the same way as a standard field. To ensure proper display, we will use stdWrap for each field in the code. Therefore, no change of the code will be required, only the template and TypoScript adjustment.

Here is what we add to res/pi1_template.html:

```
<h1>Single view</h1>
<!-- ###SINGLE_VIEW### begin -->
<div class="tx_feuserstat_single">
    <table>
        <tr><td rowspan="5">
```

```
        ###IMAGE###
      </td><td class="tx_feuserstat_label">
        ###TEXT_USERNAME###
      </td><td class="tx_feuserstat_value">
        ###FIELD_USERNAME###
      </td></tr>
      <tr><td class="tx_feuserstat_label">
        ###TEXT_NAME###
      </td><td class="tx_feuserstat_value">
        ###FIELD_NAME###
      </td></tr>
      <tr><td class="tx_feuserstat_label">
        ###TEXT_CRDATE###
      </td><td class="tx_feuserstat_value">
        ###FIELD_CRDATE###
      </td></tr>
      <tr><td class="tx_feuserstat_label">
        ###TEXT_TSTAMP###
      </td><td class="tx_feuserstat_value">
        ###FIELD_TSTAMP###
      </td></tr>
      <tr><td class="tx_feuserstat_label">
        ###TEXT_EMAIL###
      </td><td class="tx_feuserstat_value">
        ###FIELD_EMAIL###
      </td></tr>
    </table>
  </div>
<!-- ###SINGLE_VIEW### end -->
<h1>Single view when user is not found</h1>
<!-- ###SINGLE_VIEW_NO_USER### begin -->
###TEXT_USER_NOT_FOUND###
<!-- ###SINGLE_VIEW_NO_USER### end -->
```

There are two subparts: one for a "normal" single view and one for the case when the user is not found. While it is very tempting to save time and just output a single string in case the user is not found, it is always better to provide extra customization capabilities. Coding extra subsection will take another 3-5 minutes as compared to outputting a simple string, but an extension will only benefit from another subsection.

Adding stdWrap for Fields

stdWrap is a powerful way to alter presentation of the value, or render it completely differently. Our plugin will provide an excellent example of using stdWrap for such purposes. The Frontend user record will be the data for stdWrap. We add the following to static/frontend_user_list/setup.txt:

```
# stdWraps for fields in single view
singleView {
   # field: image
   image_stdWrap {
      setContentToCurrent = 1
      cObject = IMAGE
      cObject {
         file {
            import = uploads/pics/
            import.current = 1
            width = 150m
            height = 150m
         }
         imageLinkWrap = 1
         imageLinkWrap {
            enable = 1
            JSwindow = 1
         }
      }
      ifEmpty.dataWrap (
<div class="tx_feuserstat_pi1_no_image">
{LLL:EXT:feuserstat/pi1/locallang.xml:no_image}
</div>
)

   # field: email
   email_stdWrap {
      if.isFalse.current = 1
      typolink.parameter.dataWrap = mailto:{field:email}
   }
   # field: crdate
   crdate_stdWrap {
      strftime = %c
   }
   # field: tstamp
   tstamp_stdWrap {
      strftime = %c
   }
}
```

Here, we defined `stdWrap` for the `image`, `email`, `crdate`, and `strftime` fields. The image field will be wrapped with a link to open a larger image on click. Email will automatically get protection if `config.spamProtectEmailAddresses` is set. Note how it becomes automatic through the use of `stdWrap`; simply using `typolink` in `stdWrap` does the magic!

Date fields are formatted using a preferred representation of date and time for the current locale. This means that the plugin will automatically use a proper date format when the page language is changed.

Programming Single View

Single view shows one of these two views: user record, or the "not found" screen. So, the plan for the function is:

- Fetch the record.
- If the record is fetched successfully, display the data.
- If the record is not found, show the "not found" screen.

To fetch the record, we will use a function from the `t3lib_db` class named `exec_SELECTgetRows`. This function is good for fetching a small set of records. However, avoid fetching many records or records with a large amount of data. It may exhaust PHP memory.

We will select the `uid` and `pid` fields. `uid` identifies the record, and `pid` will limit the query to the proper site. If there are several sites in the same database, each with a separate Frontend user set, it will be good to ensure that only proper users are displayed. You can think about it as a security measure. Always think about such small but important issues when programming TYPO3 code.

The call is simple:

```
$rows = $GLOBALS['TYPO3_DB']->exec_SELECTgetRows('*',
        'fe_users',
        'uid=' . intval($this->piVars['showUid']) .
        ' AND ' .
        'pid=' . intval($this->conf['usersPid']) .
        $this->cObj->enableFields('fe_users'));
```

The only addition here is a call to `$this->cObj->enableFields('fe_users')`. It will ensure that the hidden, disabled, or time-limited records are not selected.

Also note that we have `intval` calls in the code. The value of the `showUid` variable was sanitized in the `init` function, but we still use `intval` here. It never hurts to have more security precautions.

Next, we code the easiest part, the "not found" message. It is typically better to have the smaller part first in the `if` statements. So, we code it like this:

```
$content = '';
if (count($rows) == 0) {
    $template = $this->cObj->getSubpart($this->templateCode,
        '###SINGLE_VIEW_NO_USER###');
    $content = $this->cObj->substituteMarker($template,
        '###TEXT_USER_NOT_FOUND###',
        $this->pi_getLL('user_not_found'));
}
```

Next, we code the long part, the normal view. Here, we will use a small trick. Since we do not modify the code each time an extension adds a field to the `fe_users` table, we need a way to find the labels for fields. The easiest way is to fetch labels from `$TCA`. It contains labels for each column. For some columns (namely for `crdate` and `tstamp`), we will provide our own labels. So, first we try to fetch our own label. If our own label is not there, we use the `$TCA` label.

Additionally, we need to exclude some sensitive fields. This will include password and BE-related fields.

Here is the next part of the code:

```
else {
    $markers = array();
    // Load fe_users table information into $TCA. We need
    // this because we will extract labels from $TCA
    t3lib_div::loadTCA('fe_users');
    // Labels in $TCA are usually in 'LLL:EXT:...' format
    // We need language object to "decode" them
    $lang = t3lib_div::makeInstance('language');
    /* @var $lang language */
    $lang->init($GLOBALS['TSFE']->lang);
    // Next we need a new instance of tslib_cObj because
    // we will pass user record as data to this cObject
    $cObj = t3lib_div::makeInstance('tslib_cObj');
    $cObj->start($rows[0], 'fe_users');
    /* @var $cObj tslib_cObj */
    // Now create marker for each field
    foreach ($rows[0] as $field => $value) {
        // Skip some sensitive fields
        if (!t3lib_div::inList('password,uc,' .
```

```
                'user_not_found,lockToDomain,TSconfig', $field)) {
            // Get label
            $label = $this->pi_getLL('field_' . $field);
            if (!$label) {
                // No local label, fetch it from $TCA
                $label = $lang->sL($GLOBALS['TCA']['fe_users']
                            ['columns'][$field]['label']);
            }
            // Fill markers
            $fieldUpper = strtoupper($field);
            $markers['###TEXT_' . $fieldUpper . '###'] = $label;
            $markers['###FIELD_' . $fieldUpper . '###'] =
                $cObj->stdWrap(htmlspecialchars($value),
                    $this->conf['singleView.']
                        [$field . '_stdWrap.']);
        }
    }
    // Get template for the subpart
    $template = $this->cObj->getSubpart($this->templateCode,
                '###SINGLE_VIEW###');
    // Create output
    $content = $this->cObj->substituteMarkerArray($template,
                $markers);
}
    return $content;
```

Note the use of htmlspecialchars. While it could be used through stdWrap, it is better to use it in the code directly to ensure that the field content is shown properly in the Frontend. The disadvantage of this method is that it does not allow HTML fields in fe_user record. If that becomes a problem, the plugin can be changed to use generic stdWrap when stdWrap for the field is not set. This, however, requires extra htmlSpecialChars for each specific stdWrap. So, using htmlspecialchars in the code is a good compromise.

This completes the development of a single view.

Creating a List View

We will have approximately the same number of steps for a list view as we had for a single view. In addition, we will make a separate function to obtain the SQL WHERE condition. This will help us to easily manage paging and search functionality.

Creating a Template

This template is more complex than the one created for the single view. It contains subparts along with plain markers.

There will be two subparts: the list item and the pager. The list item subpart is duplicated as many times as there are items. The pager subpart allows us to remove the pager when necessary.

We follow the same idea with the stdWrap processing for fields as for a single view. Here is what we have in the template:

```
<div class="tx_feuserstat_list">
   <table class="tx_feuserstat_list_users">
      <tr><th>
         ###TEXT_NUMBER###
      </th><th>
         ###TEXT_USERNAME###
      </th><th>
         ###TEXT_NAME###
      </th><th>
         ###TEXT_CRDATE###
      </th><th>
         ###TEXT_TSTAMP###
      </th><th>
         ###TEXT_LASTLOGIN###
      </th></tr>
      <!-- ###LIST_ITEM### begin -->
      <tr><td>
         ###NUMBER###
      </td><td>
         ###FIELD_USERNAME###
      </td><td>
         ###FIELD_NAME###
      </td><td>
         ###FIELD_CRDATE###
      </td><td>
         ###FIELD_TSTAMP###
      </td><td>
```

```
        ###FIELD_LASTLOGIN###
      </td></tr>
      <!-- ###LIST_ITEM### end -->
    </table>
    <!-- ###PAGER### begin -->
    <table class="tx_feuserstat_list_pager">
      <tr><td>
        ###LINK_PREV###
      </td><td>
        ###CURRENT_PAGE###
      </td><td>
        ###LINK_NEXT###
      </td></tr>
    </table>
    <!-- ###PAGER### end -->
  </div>
  <!-- ###LIST### end -->
```

The template is quite simple, and does not need to be explained in detail. This happened because our ideas were clear from the beginning, and the extension developed in a logical way.

Again, in real life, a developer should use CSS-based design, and should avoid tables. But this book is not about CSS. So we create the simplest working template possible.

Another thing that you can do well with your plugins is a page browser. Our implementation is the minimal possible one. It shows only two links (the previous and the next page) and the current page number. Obviously, it is not enough for a good looking and fully functional page browser. But the reader may want to implement a better page browser themselves as an exercise.

Modifying the TypoScript Template

TypoScript gets several adjustments. For a list view, we need to add the `stdWrap` field definitions. Additionally, we will add the page size option. It can be edited through the Constant Editor.

To change constants, we modify `static/frontend_user_list/constants.txt`. We add the following entries before the closing curly bracket:

```
# cat=feuserstat: List view; type=int+; label=Page size:
Number of items displayed on a single page in the list view
pageSize = 10
# cat=feuserstat: List view; type=string; label=Sort by:
```

A valid field from fe_users table for sorting items. Incorrect field
name field will cause empty output

```
sortField = username
```

And we add the following in `setup.txt`:

```
listViews {
        pageSize = {$plugin.tx_feuserstat_pi1.pageSize}
        sortField = {$plugin.tx_feuserstat_pi1.sortField}
        username_stdWrap {
            typolink.parameter <  plugin.tx_feuserstat_pi1.singlePid
            typolink.parameter.ifEmpty.dataWrap = {TSFE:id}
            typolink.additionalParams.dataWrap = &tx_feuserstat_
pi1[showUid]={field:uid}
        }
        email_stdWrap {
            if.isFalse.current = 1
            typolink.parameter.dataWrap = mailto:{field:email}
        }
        crdate_stdWrap {
            strftime = %x
        }
        tstamp_stdWrap {
            strftime = %x
        }
        lastlogin_stdWrap {
            strftime = %x
        }
    }
```

The `pageSize` option is populated from the constant we created in `constants.txt`.
This option is not likely to change through flexform. So we leave it in TypoScript.
The same applies to the `sortField` option.

Next, there are five `stdWrap` definitions. Date formatting is changed for a preferable
date (without time) representation of the current locale to shorten the column on
the page. The email `stdWrap` is identical to the one from the single view. The user
name field is wrapped with a link to the single view of the current record. Often,
plugin authors tend to hardcode such links to a certain field, but this method lacks
flexibility. For example, a website owner may want to link a completely different
field. Here, `stdWrap` comes of use. It can transform the field representation easily,
and without any code changes.

Programming List View

Since a list view contains more markers, subsections, and repeating elements, it is more complex than a single view. While it is possible to code everything in a single long function, we will split it into several functions. It not only enhances readability but also provides better modularity. If necessary, code in a small function can be adjusted or rewritten without any side effect on other parts of the code. Always try to split your functions into smaller logical pieces!

The plan for the list view is as follows:

- Prepare (fetch and calculate) page-related parameters.
- Fetch a template.
- Create header for the list.
- Create list rows.
- Create pager.
- Assemble everything for the output.

This looks simple enough and easy to implement. It always helps to have a plan when a function is more complex rather than just outputting "Hello world!".

The code naturally comes from the plan:

```
protected function listView() {
    // Get list parameters
    $pageSize = t3lib_div::testInt(
            $this->conf['listView.']['pageSize']) ?
                intval($this->conf['listView.']['pageSize']) :
                10;
    $page = max(1, intval($this->piVars['page']));
    // Get template for LIST view
    $template = $this->cObj->getSubpart($this->templateCode,
                    '###LIST###');
    // Get plain markers
    $markers = $this->listViewGetHeaderMarkers();
    // Get rows
    $subParts['###LIST_ITEM###'] =
        $this->listViewGetRows($template, $page, $pageSize);
    // Create pager
    $subParts['###PAGER###'] =
        $this->listViewGetPager($template, $page, $pageSize);
    // Compile output
    $content = $this->cObj->substituteMarkerArrayCached(
            $template, $markers, $subParts);
    return $content;
}
```

First, we fetch page parameters. We need to find what the page size is (how many data rows we are about to show) and what the current page number is. Both these parameters affect how many items we select, the starting item, and also what each page browser shows. As usual, we try to substitute reasonable defaults if the parameters are not set. This never hurts, but often helps if a website owner made a mistake and mistyped the parameter.

The current page is fetched from $this->piVars['page']. In the page URL, this parameter will look like tx_feuserstat_pi1[page]=7. However, this parameter is not always supplied or can be supplied incorrectly (for example, tx_feuserstat_pi1[page]=oops). Therefore, we need to validate it, and provide a default value if necessary. intval helps to convert input to integer value and max creates a default value if the parameter was not supplied.

Next in the code, we fetch the template subpart for the list view. Since it is used in more than one function, it is good to fetch it here.

Next, we call three functions to follow our plan: fetch header markers, create list rows, and create pager. Everything looks simple so far. Note the names we have for the functions. The first part of the name is always listView, which tells where the function belongs. This is one of the small details that make good code.

The last two lines combine the output of three functions into the list view.

Now, when we have a high-level list view function, let's "drill down" and create other functions.

The listViewGetHeaderMarkers function will behave like the corresponding part of the single view. However, here we do not have a database row yet, so we have to loop over the $TCA fields to fetch strings. This creates a little problem because some fields are not defined in $TCA. For them, we fill fetch titles manually. Here is the code:

```
protected function listViewGetHeaderMarkers() {
    // Prepare
    t3lib_div::loadTCA('fe_users');
    $lang = t3lib_div::makeInstance('language');
    /* @var $lang language */
    $lang->init($GLOBALS['TSFE']->lang);
    // Fill some header markers. Here we will use all
    // registered TCA fields plus
    // two date fields to add header markers
    $markers = array(
        '###TEXT_NUMBER###' => $this->pi_getLL('text_number'),
        '###TEXT_CRDATE###' =>
                $this->pi_getLL('field_crdate'),
        '###TEXT_TSTAMP###' =>
```

```
                    $this->pi_getLL('field_tstamp'),
        '###TEXT_LASTLOGIN###' =>
                    $this->pi_getLL('field_lastlogin'),
    );
    // Create markers
    foreach (array_keys(
        $GLOBALS['TCA']['fe_users']['columns']) as $field) {
        $str = $this->pi_getLL('field_' . $field);
        if (!$str) {
            $str = $lang->sL($GLOBALS['TCA']['fe_users']
                ['columns'][$field]['label']);
        }
        $markers['###TEXT_' . strtoupper($field) . '###'] =
            $str;
    }
    return $markers;
}
```

Next, we create a function that generates data rows. It is called `listViewGetRows`.

Inside this function, we need to select a certain number of user records. Selection should start from a certain item, which implies that we need to sort items to have consistent results. In the code, we will use a sorting field configured in the TypoScript setup. We must take care of the case when this field is mistyped. SQL query will not return result, and we will return empty content. But we will provide a log message to the Frontend admin panel about it.

When showing fields, we must avoid showing the same set of fields that we excluded in the single view. Since the duplicating approach is bad, we extract this value into the protected class attribute named `protectedFields`. Could this be foreseen? Probably, yes. But optimization tips do not always come into one's mind while thinking about an extension. So, if a tip suddenly pops up during development, either record it somewhere (not to forget!) or implement it straight away.

In addition to fields, we will provide a record number. This is not the same as the record's `uid` value, because some `uid` values may be missing (user deleted or disabled).

Now it is clear how we are going to implement the function. Let's do it. Here is the code:

```
protected function listViewGetRows($template, $page,
                                   $pageSize) {
    // Get parameters for database call
    $sort = $this->conf['listView.']['sortField'] ?
```

```
                    $this->conf['listView.']['sortField'] :
                    'username ASC';
        $number = ($page - 1)*$pageSize;
        // Prepare all necessary objects and arrays
        $cObj = t3lib_div::makeInstance('tslib_cObj');
        $subTemplate = $this->cObj->getSubpart($template,
                        '###LIST_ITEM###');
        /* @var $cObj tslib_cObj */
        // Get data from database
        $res = $GLOBALS['TYPO3_DB']->exec_SELECTquery('*',
                'fe_users',
                $this->getListWhere() .
                $this->cObj->enableFields('fe_users'),
                '', $sort, $number . ',' . $pageSize);
        // Collect data
        $content = '';
        // Must check if we got result. We could get null due to
        // the wrong sort field!
        if (!$res) {
            $GLOBALS['TT']->setTSlogMessage(
                    'SQL query for user records in list view has' .
                    ' failed in ' . $this->prefixId .
                    ' plugin. No users will be shown!', 2);
        }
        else {
            while (false !== ($ar =
                    $GLOBALS['TYPO3_DB']->sql_fetch_assoc($res))) {
                // Prepare for stdWrap
                $cObj->start($ar, 'fe_users');
                // Loop through fields applying stdWrap
                $subMarkers = array(
                    '###NUMBER###' => ++$number,
                );
                foreach ($ar as $field => $value) {
                    if (!t3lib_div::inList($this->protectedFields,
                                    $field)) {
                    $subMarkers['###FIELD_' .
                                strtoupper($field) . '###'] =
                        $cObj->stdWrap(htmlspecialchars($value),
                                $this->conf['listView.']
                                [$field . '_stdWrap.']);
                    }
                }
                // Add row to output
```

```
        $content .=
            $this->cObj->substituteMarkerArray($subTemplate,
                              $subMarkers);
        }
        // Free database result
        $GLOBALS['TYPO3_DB']->sql_free_result($res);
    }
    return $content;
}
```

Again, it is important to point out comments inside the function. Comments help us to understand the code. Make it a habit to write comments in your code. It takes a few extra seconds, but you will appreciate that you did it if you have to look at the code after a few months. Your ideas will be clearer to you if you record them as comments.

The function above calls the getListWhere function. As mentioned earlier, we use a dedicated function to create an SQL WHERE condition because we do not want to clutter the code of the listViewGetRows with complex SQL logic. Later, we will add search statements to this function. For now, the function is extremely simple:

```
function getListWhere() {
    return 'pid=' . intval($this->conf['usersPid']);
}
```

The last function is listViewGetPager, where we do the following:

- Check whether we need pager at all and remove it if not necessary.
- Check if we need a link to the previous page and act accordingly.
- Create page numbers.
- Check if we need a link to the next page and act accordingly.

This sounds like a good implementation plan. Let's proceed:

```
protected function listViewGetPager($template, $page,
                              $pageSize) {
    // Check if we need page at all
    list($row) = $GLOBALS['TYPO3_DB']->exec_SELECTgetRows(
            'COUNT(*) AS t',
            'fe_users',
            $this->getListWhere() .
            $this->cObj->enableFields('fe_users'));
    if ($row['t'] < $pageSize) {
        // Remove pager completely
        return '';
```

```
    }
    // Prepare
    $markers = array(
        '###CURRENT_PAGE###' => $page,
    );
    if ($page == 1) {
        // No previous page
        $markers['###LINK_PREV###'] = '';
    }
    else {
        $markers['###LINK_PREV###'] =
                $this->pi_linkTP_keepPIvars(
                $this->pi_getLL('link_prev'),
                array('page' => $page - 1), true);
    }
    if ($row['t'] <= $page*$pageSize) {
        // No next link
        $markers['###LINK_NEXT###'] = '';
    }
    else {
        $markers['###LINK_NEXT###'] =
                $this->pi_linkTP_keepPIvars(
                $this->pi_getLL('link_next'),
                array('page' => $page + 1), true);
    }
    $subTemplate = $this->cObj->getSubpart($template,
                        '###PAGER###');
    return $this->cObj->substituteMarkerArray(
                        $subTemplate, $markers);
}
```

Here, we used `t3lib_db::exec_SELECTgetRows` again because we needed a quick, small, and simple result. This function returns an association array, so we made `t` a shortcut to `COUNT(*)`. Note that we use `getListWhere` again because the pager will be used for displaying search results as well.

Next, we create page links. Here, we use a very convenient function named `pi_linkTP_keepPIvars`. This function will generate a link to the existing URL parameters of all the plugins from `$this->piVars`. It uses the first parameter as the text to link to. The second parameter tells the function which plugin parameters should be changed. We place the `page` parameter here. The last function parameter is a cache indicator. We obviously want cache, so we set it to `true` (by default, it is historically set to `false` in function definition). There are other functions like this (we have seen them in the previous chapters). At this moment, the reader is encouraged to look at what other function or functions we could use at this place in the code.

Since we are doing a sample implementation for learning purposes, we do not create a fancy looking universal page browser. In a better page browser, the next and previous links could be graphical or text (maybe through `stdWrap`) and the number of pages to show before and after the current page would be configurable.

But now we are done with the list view! Our plugin is more than half finished!

What is Missing in the List View

There are certain things that are missing in the list view. They can be implemented in the later plugin versions. Here are a few examples:

- Show a message when there are no users to show. This is important for a search view or if the page number is too high. Currently, we just show an empty list.
- Better pager. This was mentioned already.
- There is no styling.

The reader should feel capable of implementing these features now. It is good practice to implement them because there are small technical challenges in all these features.

Creating Search

Search functionality will contain a box at the top of the list view. In order to demonstrate the eID TYPO3 feature and its usage for plugins, we will also add an autocomplete feature to this box.

Including Styles and Scripts

The search box will use JavaScript and CSS styles for autocomplete. While adjusting our plugin, we added JavaScript and CSS files to the `res` directory of the extension. Now it is time to make them work.

Historically, plugins include CSS code through the `_CSS_DEFAULT_STYLE` TypoScript property in the plugin's TypoScript. The advantage of that is that these styles can be changed from the TypoScript setup or extracted to external files by TYPO3 automatically. However, there are certain disadvantages of this approach. And the disadvantages come as follow ups to the advantages.

The disadvantages are:

- TypoScript becomes less readable.
- TypoScript becomes much longer (higher parsing times, worse performance).
- If CSS styles are extracted to an external file, they will be loaded by TYPO3 regardless of the plugin's presence on the page (causes slower page rendering). Imagine if you have 10-20 plugins with long CSS or JavaScript blocks. Do you need them all on every page? Probably not.
- CSS and JavaScript are logically separated from the template, which makes them harder to modify and test.

There is a better technique, which (to the author's best knowledge) was first used in the comments extension.

The idea is to use a subpart inside the template's <head> tag to add references to the CSS and JavaScript files directly to the template. Then, the plugin can extract the subpart, substitute a path marker with a known path to the files, and add the results to the TSFE for display on the page. A developer can possibly put any additional code onto the page (javascripts, more CSS files, and so on). We will see how it works when we implement the search functionality.

This works well with USER plugins. It will also work for USER_INT plugins, but some caution should be taken. The USER_INT plugins are executed after the page generation is finished, or when the page is fetched from the cache. TSFE changes will appear on the screen only if they were added when the page was generated for caching. If the page is taken from cache, altering TSFE will not have any effect. What is the consequence of this fact? The USER_INT plugins must provide the same set of CSS/JavaScript for any of its functions on the same page. The page will be cached at the first user visit. Even if the next visit causes a different USER_INT rendering, any changes to the CSS/JavaScript will not appear on the screen. However, the CSS/JavaScript from the first visit will! Again, this happens only for the USER_INT plugins, and this should be remembered when working with these type of plugins.

How does inclusion look in practice? We shall start with template modification.

```
<head>
<title>pi1 plugin template file</title>
<!-- ###HEADER_PARTS### begin -->
<script type="text/javascript"
        src="###SITE_REL_PATH###res/pi1.js"></script>
<link rel="stylesheet" type="text/css"
        href="###SITE_REL_PATH###res/pi1.css" />
<!-- ###HEADER_PARTS### end -->
</head>
```

The added part is given in bold. This does not allow testing of styles inline. The same `<script>` and `<link>` tags can be added outside the section without `###SITE_REL_PATH###` to allow such testing.

How do we use it in the code? Here is a new function that accomplishes it:

```
function addHeaderParts() {
    $key = 'EXT:' . $this->extKey . md5($this->templateCode);
    if (!isset($GLOBALS['TSFE']->additionalHeaderData[$key])) {
        $headerParts = $this->cObj->getSubpart(
                $this->templateCode, '###HEADER_PARTS###');
        if ($headerParts) {
            $headerParts = $this->cObj->substituteMarker(
                $headerParts, '###SITE_REL_PATH###',
                t3lib_extMgm::siteRelPath($this->extKey));
            $GLOBALS['TSFE']->additionalHeaderData[$key] =
                $headerParts;
        }
    }
}
```

This function should be called from `main` after `init` is called. Alternatively, it could be placed directly inside `init`. Now, the plugin's related CSS and JavaScript will appear only on the pages where the plugin is located.

Adding a Search Box to the Template

We need the following additional code inside the `###LIST###` template subpart:

```
<!-- ###LIST### begin -->
<div class="tx_feuserstat_list">
    <form name="tx_feuserstat_list_search"
            id="tx_feuserstat_list_search"
            action="###ACTION###" method="get">
        <label for="tx_feuserstat_pi1[search]">
            ###TEXT_SEARCH###
        </label>
        <input type="text" name="tx_feuserstat_pi1[search]"
            autocomplete="off"
            id="tx_feuserstat_pi1_search"
            value="###SEARCH_TERMS###" />
        <input type="submit" name="tx_feuserstat_pi1[submit]"
            value="###TEXT_SUBMITBTN###" />
    </form>
    <table class="tx_feuserstat_list_users">
        <tr><th>
```

There are four new markers. Firstly, the ###ACTION### marker will contain the page address where the search has to be submitted. We will use the same page for search as that used for the list view (current page). In real life, the search page ID should be configurable through TypoScript and flexform, because website owners may want to have search results on differently styled or organized pages.

Next, there is a label marker (###TEXT_SEARCH###), a search terms marker (###SEARCH_TERMS###), and a marker for button text (###TEST_SUBMITBTN###).

Adding a Search Condition

The search condition is added to the getListWhere function. We will search the username and name fields. Search will start from the beginning of the name. The function transforms to:

```
function getListWhere() {
    $where = 'pid=' . intval($this->conf['usersPid']);
    if (($search = trim($this->piVars['search']))) {
        $search = $GLOBALS['TYPO3_DB']->fullQuoteStr(
                    $search . '%', 'fe_users');
        $where .= ' AND (username LIKE ' . $search .
                    ' OR name LIKE ' . $search . ')';
    }
    return $where;
}
```

What About Cache?

Now, we hit a significant problem. Our plugin is USER (cached). It requires cHash because it accepts parameters. But we cannot calculate cHash for search because a user enters a random search string. So, we have a problem with caching. What do we do?

The simplest solution is to add a hidden field to the HTML template. The field is named no_cache and its value is 1. It will prevent page cache for the next request. This is typically how the problem of user submission is solved. But this solution is bad (as shown in the previous chapter of this book) because it disables caching for the whole page and seriously decreases performance.

Another temptation is to convert the plugin to USER_INT. This is certainly a solution. However, converting the plugin from cached to noncached because of the search function, does not look right.

How do we solve it? We can solve this problem if we remember why we have the problem. It happens because of the missing cHash when we search. So, if we search without a cHash, we need non-cached output from the plugin. If we search with a cHash, we need cached output.

How do we implement it? It is easy using TypoScript conditions and a small piece of PHP code in the plugin.

First, we add the following to TypoScript at the end of setup.txt:

```
[globalString = GP:tx_feuserstat_pi1|search = /.+/] &&
[globalString = GP:cHash = /^$/]
plugin.tx_feuserstat_pi1 = USER_INT
[global]
```

 The first two lines in the code example above must be actually on a single line.

This makes our plugin USER_INT when the search string is not empty and there is no cHash. Easy!

Next, we have to create a constructor inside tx_feuserstat_pi1 to reset $this->pi_checkCHash if we are running as USER_INT:

```
function __construct() {
    if (empty($GLOBALS['TSFE']->cHash)) {
        // Might be USER_INT case
        $piVars = t3lib_div::GParrayMerged($this->prefixId);
        if ($piVars['search']) {
            $this->pi_checkCHash = false;
        }
    }
    parent::tslib_pibase();
}
```

This fixes cache problems for our extension.

The technique demonstrated in this section is not common. But it shows that many problems can be solved in a better way than in the obvious way. When a developer hits the problem, he / she should not rush with the first obvious solution. Maybe there is a better solution available.

Creating JavaScript for Autocomplete

For JavaScript autocomplete, we will use Prototype and Scriptaculous frameworks supplied with TYPO3. This is the easiest way, and does not need any standalone libraries other than those provided by TYPO3 already.

We will not go deep into the details on this JavaScript. If the reader wants to know more about it, detailed examples can be found on Scriptaculous website. Both the JavaScript and styles are very close to those in the official examples.

The JavaScript is as follows:

```
function tx_feuserstat_pi1_init(ctrlId, acId, pid) {
    document.observe('dom:loaded', function() {
        new Ajax.Autocompleter(ctrlId, acId, 'index.php', {
            parameters: 'eID=feuserstat&pid=' + pid,
            paramName: 'search'
        });
    });
}
```

A template also needs changes. First, Prototype and Scriptaculous should be added:

```
<!-- ###HEADER_PARTS### begin -->
<script type="text/javascript" src="typo3/contrib/prototype/
prototype.js"></script>
<script type="text/javascript" src="typo3/contrib/
scriptaculous/scriptaculous.js"></script>
<script type="text/javascript" src="typo3/contrib/
scriptaculous/controls.js"></script>
<script type="text/javascript" src="###SITE_REL_PATH###res/pi1.js"></
script>
<link rel="stylesheet" type="text/css" href="###SITE_REL_PATH###res/
pi1.css" />
<!-- ###HEADER_PARTS### end -->
```

Next, we modify the search form:

```
<form name="tx_feuserstat_list_search"
     id="tx_feuserstat_list_search" action="###ACTION###"
     method="get">
  <label for="tx_feuserstat_pi1[search]">
     ###TEXT_SEARCH###
  </label>
  <input type="text" name="tx_feuserstat_pi1[search]"
     id="tx_feuserstat_pi1_search" autocomplete="off"
     value="###SEARCH_TERMS###" />
  <div id="tx_feuserstat_pi1_autoc"></div>
  <input type="submit" name="tx_feuserstat_pi1[submit]"
     value="###TEXT_SUBMITBTN###" />
  <script type="text/javascript">
     tx_feuserstat_pi1_init('tx_feuserstat_pi1_search',
        'tx_feuserstat_pi1_autoc', ###PID###)
  </script>
</form>
```

We need the ###PID### marker because we must pass it to our server-side
AJAX part for proper user filtering. We create this marker in the
listViewGetHeaderMarkers function:

```
$markers = array(
    '###TEXT_NUMBER###' => $this->pi_getLL('text_number'),
    '###TEXT_CRDATE###' =>
        $this->pi_getLL('field_crdate'),
    '###TEXT_TSTAMP###' =>
        $this->pi_getLL('field_tstamp'),
    '###TEXT_LASTLOGIN###' =>
        $this->pi_getLL('field_lastlogin'),
    '###TEXT_SEARCH###' =>
        $this->pi_getLL('text_search'),
    '###TEXT_SUBMITBTN###' =>
        $this->pi_getLL('text_submitbtn'),
    '###ACTION###' =>
        $this->pi_getPageLink($GLOBALS['TSFE']->id),
    '###SEARCH_TERMS###' =>
        htmlspecialchars($this->piVars['search']),
    '###PID###' => intval($this->conf['usersPid']),
);
```

CSS changes are directly copied from the Scriptaculous tutorial, so we do not show
them here.

This completes the JavaScript and CSS changes for adding autocomplete. Now, we
should create a server-side script that provides autocomplete data.

Creating PHP Code for Autocomplete

We have a dummy file and PHP class for the AJAX call. The file is named
tx_feuserstat_eID and located in class.tx_feuserstat_eid.php.

eID scripts are scripts inside TYPO3 framework that have access to most basic
TYPO3 services (such as database or t3lib_extMgm). Most of the TYPO3 framework
is not initialized and classes like tslib_cObj are not available.

eID scripts are much faster than regular TYPO3 pages. However, they are much
trickier to program. As we will see, even a simple database query requires additional
code to emulate tslib_cObj::enableFields functionality. This is one of the
reasons why eID scripts are not very common.

Our eID class will have only the function named `main`. Its purpose is to fetch a maximum of 100 records of matching users and return them in the Scriptaculous-compatible format (which, in this case, is an unordered HTML list). The function must be called by us in the same file. TYPO3 simply includes eID script file and assumes that output will be provided.

We create the following code after the XCLASS declaration in the file:

```
$SOBE = t3lib_div::makeInstance('tx_feuserstat_eID');
$SOBE->main();
```

It is important to place this code after the XCLASS declaration to ensure that XCLASSing still works.

Next, we create the `main` function:

```
function main() {
   // Connect database
   tslib_eidtools::connectDB();
   // Get query parameters
   $pid = intval(t3lib_div::_GP('pid'));
   $search = trim(t3lib_div::_GP('search'));
   // Get content
   $content = '';
   if ($pid && strlen($search) >= 3) {
      // Prepare & execute search, 100 items max
      $qsearch = $GLOBALS['TYPO3_DB']->fullQuoteStr(
            $search . '%', 'fe_users');
      $res = $GLOBALS['TYPO3_DB']->exec_SELECTquery(
         'username,name',
         'fe_users', 'pid=' . $pid .
         ' AND (username LIKE ' . $qsearch .
         ' OR name LIKE ' . $qsearch . ')' .
         t3lib_BEfunc::deleteClause('fe_users') .
         t3lib_BEfunc::BEenableFields('fe_users'),
         '', '', 100);
      $result = array();
      while (false !== ($ar =
            $GLOBALS['TYPO3_DB']->sql_fetch_assoc($res))) {
         // Record only matching values
         foreach ($ar as $value) {
            if (stristr($value, $search) !== false) {
               $result[] = $value;
            }
         }
      }
      $GLOBALS['TYPO3_DB']->sql_free_result($res);
```

```
    // Sort results and create content
    if (count($result)) {
        sort($result);
         $content = '<li>' .
             implode('</li><li>', $result) . '</li>';
    }
}
    // Output result
    echo '<ul> ' . $content . '</ul>';
}
```

First, we connect to the database. Remember that TYPO3 does not do that automatically for eID scripts. Next, we get query parameters and check if we have at least three symbols to search for. It does not make sense to search for fewer symbols.

Next, we perform the search. Here comes the interesting part. Since we do not have `tslib_cObj::enableFields` here, we have to "invent" some other way to achieve the same effect. Fortunately, we can use Backend functions. This is not really a clean way, but currently there is no other way at all for eID. Note that we have to call two separate BE functions to do the same job that `tslib_cObj::enableFields` does.

To use these functions, the top of the file has to contain the following lines:

```
 * Hint: use extdeveval to insert/update function index above.
 */
require_once(PATH_t3lib . 'class.t3lib_befunc.php');
require_once(PATH_t3lib . 'stddb/tables.php');
require_once(t3lib_extMgm::extPath('cms', 'ext_tables.php'));
/**
 * Handles AJAX request from tx_feuserstat_pi1 plugin
 */
class tx_feuserstat_eID {
```

Additionally, we manually include the $TCA definition scripts (TYPO3 does not do it for eID either).

Now, search can be tried with autocomplete.

Adding Hooks

It is generally a good idea to give fellow programmers a chance to extend your extension even further. Often such a task can be done by providing hooks.

Hooks are functions that are registered with the extension and called by extensions at the appropriate moments of code execution with the appropriate purpose.

Hooks are registered in the `ext_localconf.php` file:

```
$TYPO3_CONF_VARS['EXTCONF']['feuserstat']
    ['extraItemMarkers'][$_EXTKEY] =
        'EXT:' . $_EXTKEY .
        '/class.tx_myext_hooks.php:tx_myext_hooks->hookFunc';
```

The plugin will loop over each entry and call the corresponding function using `t3lib_div::callUserFunc`.

We will have two hooks in our plugin for adding or changing markers:

- Hook for the single and list view.
- Hook for the plain markers in the list view.

Each hook will pass an array of parameters to the hook function. This array will consist of the following elements:

Name	Type	Description
markers	array	Array with markers. Hook can either add or change markers and must return the modified array.
pObj	tx_feuserstat_pi1	Reference to the calling class.

The advantage of passing parameters this way is that new parameters can be easily added in future without creating compatibility problems with existing hooks.

The hook function will access and modify markers in the following way:

```
function hookFunc(array $params, tx_feuserstat_pi1 &$pObj) {
    $markers = &$params['markers'];
    $markers['###TX_MYEXT_UNIXTIME###'] = time();
    return $markers;
}
```

Note that the hook function here uses a marker name that includes the hook's extension key. This is a good way to prevent marker name conflicts.

First, we add the hook to `singleView`:

```
                $markers['###FIELD_' . $fieldUpper . '###'] =
                    $cObj->stdWrap(htmlspecialchars($value),
                    $this->conf['singleView.']
                    [$field . '_stdWrap.']);
            }
        }
        // Call hooks
```

```
if (isset($GLOBALS['TYPO3_CONF_VARS']['EXTCONF']
        [$this->extKey]['extraItemMarkers'])) {
    foreach ($GLOBALS['TYPO3_CONF_VARS']
            ['EXTCONF'][$this->extKey]
            ['extraItemMarkers'] as $userFunc) {
        $params = array(
            'markers' => $markers,
            'pObj' => &$this,
        );
        $markers = t3lib_div::callUserFunction(
            $userFunc, $params, $this);
    }
}
$template = $this->cObj->getSubpart(
        $this->templateCode, '###SINGLE_VIEW###');
$content = $this->cObj->substituteMarkerArray(
        $template, $markers);
```

The same piece of code is added to `listViewGetRows`:

```
foreach ($ar as $field => $value) {
    if (!t3lib_div::inList($this->protectedFields,
        $field)) {
        $subMarkers['###FIELD_' .
            strtoupper($field) . '###'] =
            $cObj->stdWrap(htmlspecialchars($value),
                $this->conf['listView.'][$field .
                '_stdWrap.']);
    }
}
// Call hooks
if (isset($GLOBALS['TYPO3_CONF_VARS']['EXTCONF']
        [$this->extKey]['extraItemMarkers'])) {
    foreach ($GLOBALS['TYPO3_CONF_VARS']
            ['EXTCONF'][$this->extKey]
            ['extraItemMarkers'] as $userFunc) {
        $params = array(
            'markers' => $markers,
            'pObj' => &$this,
        );
        $markers = t3lib_div::callUserFunction(
            $userFunc, $params, $this);
    }
}
// Add a row to output
$content .= $this->cObj->substituteMarkerArray(
    $subTemplate, $subMarkers);
```

The Hook for the plain markers is added to `listViewGetHeaderMarkers`:

```
// Create markers
foreach (array_keys($GLOBALS['TCA']['fe_users']
        ['columns']) as $field) {
    $str = $this->pi_getLL('field_' . $field);
    if (!$str) {
        $str = $lang->sL($GLOBALS['TCA']['fe_users']
        ['columns'][$field]['label']);
    }
    $markers['###TEXT_' . strtoupper($field) . '###'] =
        $str;
}
// Call hooks
if (isset($GLOBALS['TYPO3_CONF_VARS']['EXTCONF']
        [$this->extKey]['extraGlobalMarkers'])) {
    foreach ($GLOBALS['TYPO3_CONF_VARS']
        ['EXTCONF'][$this->extKey]
        ['extraGlobalMarkers'] as $userFunc) {
    $params = array(
        'markers' => $markers,
        'pObj' => &$this,
    );
    $markers = t3lib_div::callUserFunction(
        $userFunc, $params, $this);
    }
}
return $markers;
```

This completes the hook creation. Now, any extension can add or change our markers, which enhances the plugin's flexibility significantly.

What Can Be Optimized?

After creating the plugin, it is good to look into the code and see what could be optimized. Our code is simple, and there is not much room for optimization.

One thing that we could do is to create a constructor for the class, make `$lang` a class attribute, and move its creation there (`$lang` is always used in both list and single views). Would this be an optimization? Yes and no. It is true that it is created in both functions. However, in the list view, it is used only for header labels. Having it as a class attribute is an additional memory overhead. So currently, we keep it local. However, we could still do better by making a separate function for creating `$lang`. This is left for the reader as another exercise.

Another optimization is to enhance error reporting by using the `t3lib_div::devLog` function in addition to `$GLOBALS['TT']->setTSlogMessage`. It never hurts to provide better logging. For that, we should create another dedicated logging function and call it instead of calling `$GLOBALS['TT']->setTSlogMessage`. Inside such a function, we should call `$GLOBALS['TT']->setTSlogMessage` and `t3lib_div::devLog`. We leave this exercise to the reader.

Summary

In this chapter, we learned how to create a Frontend plugin. We learned how to create configuration, different views, and how to handle cache issues. We also programmed an eID script, which is one of the lesser known aspects of TYPO3. Now the reader can create his own Frontend plugins.

7
Programming Backend Modules

In this chapter, we will learn how to program Backend modules. In addition, we will create several classes that gather information displayed by a Backend module. These classes will be hooks to TYPO3 TSFE objects (page object). This is the final chapter on programming in the book.

Planning a Backend Module

As usual, we will plan before implementation. The advantages of planning have already been discussed in the previous chapters, and we will take this topic up again.

Functionality of a Backend Module

Kickstarter generated a sample Backend module for us. The module is available under the **Web** main module in the left menu. We will show the following information in the module:

- Fixed number of latest logins. For each login, we will show the following:
    - Date and time of the login
    - How much time a user spends on the site
    - User real name (`name` column in the `fe_users` table)
    - User login name (`username` column in the `fe_users` table)
    - The number of pages visited

- Monthly view shows all logins for up to the last 12 months. Each month shows:
  - ○ User real name
  - ○ User login name
  - ○ Number of logins in the current month

- Active users report shows active users for the given period of time. We show:
  - ○ User login name
  - ○ User name
  - ○ User email (clickable, linked to "mailto" for this user)
  - ○ Last login time

- Inactive users (same view as for Active users)

Our module does the same work that a very old TYPO3 extension named `loginusertrack` does. That extension still works, but it was written a long time ago and uses methods that are now discouraged as it creates problems for TYPO3. We will make a completely fresh implementation of this module using only the recommended methods and approaches.

Frontend Classes

To show information, we need to gather it first. We need a place that is called every time a user visits a page. Since TYPO3 normally fetches a cached version of the page, we must find a hook that is called for both cached and noncached versions.

The hook works globally (for any web page in the page tree). Sometimes, it is not necessary. Moreover, the INSERT and UPDATE queries may lower the performance of the website a little. So, we should provide a way to enable and disable our functionality. We will do it by using a new `config.tx_feuserstat_enable` TypoScript option. By default, it is disabled, and the administrator needs to enable it explicitly by setting the value of the option to 1.

The place to search for a hook calling point is `typo3/sysext/cms`. We start looking from `index_ts.php`. This is the file, which calls various TSFE functions to create output. After examining the various called methods, it seems that the `checkDataSubmission` method of TSFE is the best one – it has a hook and it is always called. Also, this function can access the TypoScript setup, which we need due to the use of the **config.tx_feuserstat_enable** TypoScript option. Not every function can access TypoScript but this function can. Without this option, we could use a hook in the `initFEUser` function. While the `checkDataSubmission` hook was intended for a different purpose, there is nothing wrong in using it for our purposes. So, we will use this place to record Frontend user statistics.

Database Structure

To record statistics, we need two database tables. The first page will record information about user sessions. The second table will record the number of hits for each page visited during the session.

In the first table, we need the following fields:

- User uid value (link to `fe_users` table)
- Session start time
- Time when the last page was hit
- Number of hits for the session
- Enter page
- Exit page

Entries in this table will correspond to our own "user sessions". The second table will contain a link to this table and other fields:

- "Session" uid (the link to the first table)
- User uid value. We could fetch it from the first table by joining two tables, but this would add extra overhead to SQL queries. So, it is much better to store the user uid here too.
- Visited page id
- Number of hits for this page

These two tables were created for us by Kickstarter when we generated the extension. So, there is very little we need to do.

Adjusting the Database

Let's review the generated code and decide if we need to change anything.

The table information is spread among three files. We start from the SQL definitions and continue to the TYPO3 definitions.

ext_tables.sql

The first file is `ext_tables.sql`. It contains SQL definitions for our new tables. Kickstarter generated SQL statements that are generally suitable for most cases. However, generated statements are not optimal. Kickstarter used `text` and `tinytext` fields where we could use the `int` fields. This will minimize the database size and let us receive the database query results faster. So, we change field definitions according to the following:

Table name	Field name	Old type	New type
tx_feuserstat_sessions	fe_user	text	int(11) DEFAULT '0' NOT NULL
	first_page	text	int(11) DEFAULT '0' NOT NULL
	last_page	text	int(11) DEFAULT '0' NOT NULL
tx_feuserstat_pagestats	fe_user	text	int(11) DEFAULT '0' NOT NULL
	sesstat_uid	text	int(11) DEFAULT '0' NOT NULL
	page_uid	text	int(11) DEFAULT '0' NOT NULL

Additionally, we remove the following three fields in each table:

- `crdate`
- `cruser_id`
- `tstamp`

We do not need these fields.

ext_tables.php

This file contains the TCA *declaration* for our tables. TCA stands for **Table Configuration Array**. TYPO3 uses TCA to determine various characteristics of the table. For example, TYPO3 can find answers to the following questions from the TCA:

- What is the table name (shown in **Web | List** module)?
- How many items are to be shown in the **Web | List** module?
- Which field is to be used as a "label" field?
- Should the table be shown at all?
- Can the table be modified?

- Can the table be placed on any page or only on some page types?
- What are the table fields?
- How do we show each field (for example, as plain input or selector box)?
- How should we group the fields?
- Should any other table be updated automatically when this table is updated?

This list is incomplete. It shows only most common uses of TCA. TYPO3 can extract much more information from the TCA when necessary.

The complete description of the TCA can be found in the **TYPO3 Core API** document available at the **Documentation** section of the http://typo3.org/ website.

TCA declaration is different from TCA definition. Declaration includes only the ctrl section of TCA. Definition includes the full TCA.

TCA definitions can be very long and take a lot of memory. There can be hundreds of extensions in the system, each defining additional tables. Having TCA definitions in the memory for every extension is not a very effective approach. Therefore, TYPO3 requires only a small part of the TCA to be included for each table. The rest of the TCA can be loaded, if necessary, on demand.

TCA is divided into several sections. Each section is just an array. For example, a typical TCA looks like this:

```
$TCA['tx_myext_table'] = array(
    'ctrl' => array(
        . . .
    ),
    'columns' => array(
        . . .
    ),
    'types' => array(
        . . .
    ),
);
```

Here, ctrl, columns, and types are sections. To declare the TCA, an extension author needs to create a ctrl section in ext_tables.php and point to where the rest of the TCA is located (usually in tca.php).

Let's see how `tx_feuserstat_sessions` is declared. The `ext_tables.php` file contains the following code:

```
$TCA['tx_feuserstat_sessions'] = array (
    'ctrl' => array (
        'title'         => 'LLL:EXT:feuserstat/locallang_db.xml:
tx_feuserstat_sessions',
        'label'         => 'uid',
        'tstamp'    => 'tstamp',
        'crdate'    => 'crdate',
        'cruser_id' => 'cruser_id',
        'default_sortby' => "ORDER BY crdate",
        'dynamicConfigFile' => t3lib_extMgm::extPath($_EXTKEY) .
                'tca.php',
        'iconfile'  => t3lib_extMgm::extRelPath($_EXTKEY) .
                'icon_tx_feuserstat_sessions.gif',
    ),
);
```

Here, we can see several options:

- Title declaration, which is normally a reference to `locallang_db.xml`.
- Label declaration, set to `uid` field because we do not have any other useful field to represent the record.
- Four lines that refer to deleted fields (`crdate`, etc).
- The `dynamicConfigFile` option to tell TYPO3 where the rest of the TCA is located.
- Table icon path. This icon will be displayed next to the table title when creating new records in the Backend for the table.

We need to remove four lines that refer to the deleted fields for both the tables. We also add two more options to each table:

```
'readOnly' => true,
'hideTable' => true
```

These two options will hide the table from the Backend and prevent its modification if the table is forcefully shown through TSConfig. We do not want anyone to manipulate statistics.

tca.php

This file defines the rest of the TCA. When the file is included, the TCA for this extension is overridden completely. Therefore, TCA needs to include the previously defined `ctrl` section. Next, other sections are defined. The only other mandatory sections are `columns` and `types`. `columns` define which columns are present in the database and how to present them in Backend forms. `types` defines the order of the columns, and how to group them. Additional fields can be specified in the `palettes` section.

Columns

All TCA column types are described in the **TYPO3 Core API** document. Let's see some examples. The **TYPO3 Core API** document should be open. Keep looking up properties there, while we discuss various TCA properties.

Here is how the `fe_users` column is defined:

```
'fe_user' => array(
    'exclude' => 1,
    'label' => 'LLL:EXT:feuserstat/locallang_db.xml:tx_
feuserstat_sessions.fe_user',
    'config' => array(
        'type' => 'group',
        'internal_type' => 'db',
        'allowed' => 'fe_users',
        'size' => 1,
        'minitems' => 0,
        'maxitems' => 1,
    )
),
```

What do we see here? It is an exclude field. Exclude fields can be protected ("excluded") from being edited by users. Since our table is hidden in the Backend and made read-only, we can remove this declaration.

Next comes `label`. It will be displayed above the field in the Backend form and in the exclude field list in the user record.

After `label`, we see the `config` array. The first property in the `config` array is `type`. It defines the field type. The **TYPO3 Core API** document describes which properties a developer can use for each type. If a property is listed for one type and not listed for another, it will not work in another type. This is an important thing to remember. Mailing lists show that developers often try to reuse options from other types. It does not work. Only use listed properties!

In the case of the `fe_user` field of our table, the type is defined as `group`. Checking the **TYPO3 Core API** document reveals that the group fields are either database relations, file relations, or folder relations. And some options are again different if the field is for the database or for the file. This different field set situation is unique to the `group` field type only. All other types have "stable" sets of fields.

The `fe_user` field has `internal_type` set to `db`. So, when we define such fields, we look for "db-only" or common options in the **TYPO3 core API** document. We ignore options for `file internal_type`.

The only `db`-specific option here is `allowed`. Looking at the **TYPO3 Core API** document reveals that it defines a table list. Records from these tables can be referenced in this field. In our case, it is only the `fe_users` table. Since we have only one table and one relation, we can do certain optimizations here. As you should remember, the `group` fields can store database relations in two formats: with table name and without. The first format is used when `allowed` lists more than one table. The SQL definition requires a string field for relations where multiple tables can be referenced. For single table and single value relations, it is enough and more optimal to have integer fields in the database.

We have already changed `ext_tables.sql` to use an integer field for `fe_user`. Now we need to tell TYPO3 to avoid the long relation syntax. In other words, TYPO3 should not prepend the table name to record `uid`. We do it by adding a new option to the column definition:

```
'config' => array(
    'type' => 'group',
    'internal_type' => 'db',
    'allowed' => 'fe_users',
    'prepend_tname' => false,
    'size' => 1,
    'minitems' => 0,
    'maxitems' => 1,
)
```

The remaining three options define how the Backend form will show the field. It is not important in our case because we hide the tables but we should still have correct settings. It is just a good style to code everything properly.

The size of the control is set to `1` because we have a single item always. Next, TCA says that `minitems` is `0` and `maxitems` is `1`. While `maxitems` is correct, `minitems` is not. We change `minitems` to become `1`. We can immediately do the same for the `first_page` and `last_page` fields.

The next two fields are `session_start` and `session_end`. They define when a session has started and finished respectively. We could easily keep the `crdate` and `tstamp` fields for this purpose, but it will not be obvious in the code why they are used and when.

Both these fields have the `eval` property. This property is one of those which developers try to use with the other types. At the moment of writing this book, the `eval` property worked only with the `input` and `text` types. `eval` sets our two fields to the required date/time. The full list of evaluations is available in the **TYPO3 Core API** document. Developers can also provide their own evaluations by writing PHP functions and registering them with TYPO3. See the **TYPO3 Core API** document for more information.

Our two date fields miss a default value. This causes a problem in TYPO3 if fields are not defined as required, do not have default value and have any date or time evaluations. TYPO3 refuses to save empty date/time fields when all these conditions are met. So, always either specify a default value (zero will do) or make this field a required field.

Next comes the `hits` field. It has a long declaration, and we will need to make several adjustments here.

First, there are `size` and `max` properties. The first property defines the size of the input field. The second defines how many characters can be entered. Usually, `size` should be set to `max` plus two characters because of browser bugs. We therefore change `size` to `6`.

Next is the `checkbox` property. It can be either empty, or should have a value. If it is empty, unchecking the checkbox in the form will remove the value in the input control. Checking the checkbox will not restore the value. But if the value of `checkbox` is not empty, checking the checkbox causes this value to appear in the control. We change the value to `1`.

Next goes the `range` specification. Kickstarter generates `10` and `1000` as a range to provide an example. We need to remove `upper` range definition completely and set `lower` to `1`.

The last property for this field is `default`. According to the **TYPO3 Core API** document, it gives a default value for the field. We set it to `1` instead of `0`.

Similar updates should be made in the second table for every field. Try performing them yourself, and compare your changes to the description above or to the downloaded code for this chapter. If something is different, think why and correct mistakes (if any).

Types

types is a powerful property, but tricky to configure. Many developers leave it as it is. Often, it is possible to create a much better representation of data in the Backend forms by adjusting types.

The types section consists of an array of arrays. The number of arrays inside this section depends on the presence of the type field in the record. The type field defines how the Backend form will look. The most known example is a content element type. When the content element is changed, the form is reloaded and a different set of fields is shown.

The type field is defined in the ctrl section of TCA (check the **TYPO3 Core API** document on how to define the type field). Each value of the type field is a key in the types section. If the type field is missing in the database, 0 is assumed to be the value of the type field. This value points to an array with another key/value pair. The key there is always the showitem. Value is what interests us the most here.

The value is a comma-separated list of field definitions. In the simplest case, field definition is just a field name or --div-- (separator).

Each field definition can contain further information separated by a semicolon. The simplest is --div--; the string after the semicolon is a label for this separator (or a reference to the label in the language file). If dividersToTabs is activated in the ctrl section of the table, this separator becomes a tab with a given label.

With nondivider fields, there can be up to four additional pieces of data. All of them are optional. These pieces are:

- Alternative label
  No one uses it these days. It supports only the old "language-split" syntax which is already obsolete. This syntax requires pipe-separated strings in different languages, a certain order and mixed character encodings. In other words, avoid it.

- Palette number
  When the option to show palettes is checked, additional fields appear below this field. See the next section on palettes.

- Special configuration
  This can be used to disable wrap on the text element or to convert a text area into the RTE text field. See the **TYPO3 Core API | Special Configuration options** section.

- Form style codes
  In the early TYPO3 days, it defined how form fields are grouped and coded by color. Currently, colors are defined by Backend skin, and grouping is the only one that is really used.

  Typically, values such as `1-1-1` or `2-2-2` are seen in form style codes. This allows us to visually separate some items from others without creating large separators by `--div--`. Again, the **TYPO3 Core API** document will provide a lot of historical and practical information about these values.

Palettes

Palettes are very similar to types. They are shown below the field that refers to the corresponding palette, and they do not have additional information as regular fields. Typically, start/stop time and Frontend user group go to the palette, which is attached to the "Hidden" flag.

The following screenshot shows record configuration with palettes disabled (*Yet Another Feed Importer* TYPO3 extension by the author of this book):

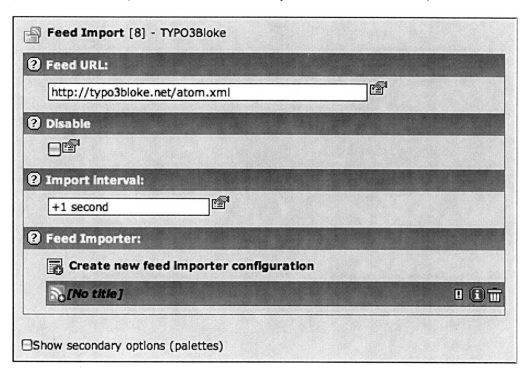

The next screenshot shows the same record but with palettes open:

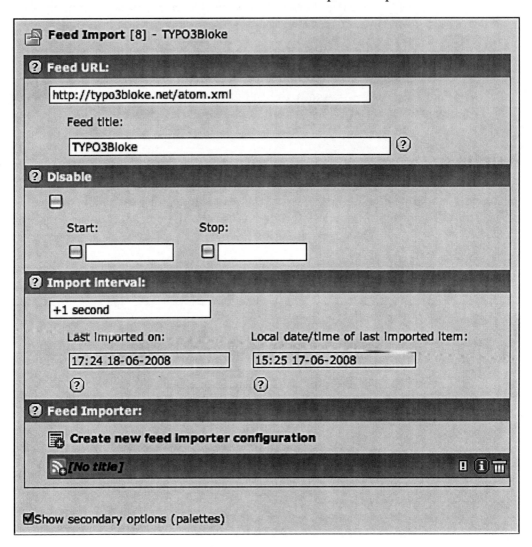

This concludes our review of TCA.

Implementing a Frontend Hook

The Frontend hook class file goes into the extension's directory. The file is named `class.tx_feuserstat_hooks.php`. According to coding conventions, the class name becomes `tx_feuserstat_hooks`. There will be only one hook inside but we name the file (and the class) in plural to enable adding more hooks if necessary in future versions.

When adding this class, GPL and XCLASS declarations should be added manually. Make sure you do this first thing after creating a new class for TYPO3.

Now, we create a dummy function for the hook. The function name has to be `checkDataSubmission` because it is hard-coded like this in the TSFE.

The TSFE provides a reference to itself as a parameter to the hook function. The same reference is available as `$GLOBALS['TSFE']`. For better clarity, we will use the global variable and will skip the function parameter completely.

Next, we need to register the hook. We do it by adding the following code to `ext_localconf.php`:

```
$GLOBALS['TYPO3_CONF_VARS']['SC_OPTIONS']
    ['tslib/class.tslib_fe.php']
    ['checkDataSubmission'][$_EXTKEY] = 'EXT:' . $_EXTKEY .
    '/class.tx_loginusertrack_tsfehook.php:' .
    'tx_loginusertrack_tsfehook';
```

In general, the way to register a hook can be found where the hook is called. For example, in the TSFE, the hook is called in the following way:

```
// Hook for processing data submission to extensions:
if (is_array($this->TYPO3_CONF_VARS['SC_OPTIONS']
    ['tslib/class.tslib_fe.php']['checkDataSubmission']))    {
    foreach($this->TYPO3_CONF_VARS['SC_OPTIONS']
    ['tslib/class.tslib_fe.php']['checkDataSubmission'] as
$_classRef)       {
        $_procObj = &t3lib_div::getUserObj($_classRef);
        $_procObj->checkDataSubmission($this);
    }
}
```

(The code above is reformatted to fit the book layout)

The hook will perform one of the following tasks:

- If a user is just logged in, we create a new session record.
- If user has logged in previously, we update session data.

In both the cases, we also insert or update information about page hits. We also need to store information about the current session inside the user object (available until logged out).

We start implementation by defining three empty functions inside our hook class:

```
public function checkDataSubmission() {
}
function createSession() {
}
function updateSession() {
}
```

As usual, we break implementation into small observable units. It helps to keep code clean, maintainable, and to help fix an error much faster and easier. We also add as many comments as needed to understand what is going on. The implementation of the checkDataSubmission checks if user tracking is enabled, and if the user is logged in. If both the conditions are met, it checks if the user is just logged in. If yes, it calls createSession, otherwise it calls updateSession. Here is how we implement this function:

```
public function checkDataSubmission() {
    // Check if statistics are enabled
    if ($GLOBALS['TSFE']->config
                ['config']['tx_feuserstat_enable']) {
        // Check if user is logged in
        if (is_array($GLOBALS['TSFE']->fe_user->user))      {
            // If user is just logged in, then create the
            // session. Otherwise update it.
            if (t3lib_div::GPvar('logintype') == 'login')    {
                $this->createSession();
            } else {
                $this->updateSession();
            }
        }
    }
}
```

The createSession function creates a new session record at the same page where the the user records are located. When the user logs in, this information is available from the pid parameter in the GET or POST data. We will use the t3lib_div::_GP API function to retrieve this parameter. It examines both GET and POST.

The uid and pid of the record will be stored in the current user record. When the user navigates through the pages, we will quickly find our session information from the user record.

Another task for the createSession function is to create an entry in the page statistics table.

And the final thing we want to do is to ensure that TYPO3 knows about our references to various tables. We will use t3lib_refindex to update this information.

Now, once we know what to do, we proceed to implementation. The code looks like this:

```
function createSession() {
    // Add session statistics
    // Extract storage pid for users
    $pid = t3lib_div::_GP('pid');
    // Fill-in field array
    $fields = array(
        'pid' => $pid,
        'fe_user' => intval(
            $GLOBALS['TSFE']->fe_user->user['uid']),
        'session_start' => $GLOBALS['SIM_EXEC_TIME'],
        'session_end' => $GLOBALS['SIM_EXEC_TIME'],
        'first_page' => $GLOBALS['TSFE']->id,
        'last_page' => $GLOBALS['TSFE']->id,
    );
    $GLOBALS['TYPO3_DB']->exec_INSERTquery(
        'tx_feuserstat_sessions', $fields);
    $sesstat_uid = $GLOBALS['TYPO3_DB']->sql_insert_id();
    $GLOBALS['TSFE']->fe_user->setKey('ses',
            self::SESSION_KEY, array(
                'pid' => $pid,
                'session_uid' => $sesstat_uid
        ));
    // Add page statistics
    $fields = array(
        'pid' => $pid,
        'fe_user' => intval(
            $GLOBALS['TSFE']->fe_user->user['uid']),
        'crdate' => $GLOBALS['SIM_EXEC_TIME'],
        'tstamp' => $GLOBALS['SIM_EXEC_TIME'],
        'page_uid' => $GLOBALS['TSFE']->id,
        'sesstat_uid' => $sesstat_uid,
    );
```

```
$GLOBALS['TYPO3_DB']->exec_INSERTquery(
    'tx_loginusertrack_pagestat', $fields);
$pagestat_uid = $GLOBALS['TYPO3_DB']->sql_insert_id();
// Uodate reference index
$ref = t3lib_div::makeInstance('t3lib_refindex');
/* @var $ref t3lib_refindex */
$ref->updateRefIndexTable('tx_feuserstat_sessions',
    $sesstat_uid);
$ref->updateRefIndexTable('tx_loginusertrack_pagestat',
    $pagestat_uid);
}
```

The updateSession function is a little more complex. First, it needs to extract the session ID from the user data. If no such ID exists, it means that the user is either not logged in, or he/she has logged in before the statistics gathering for this website was enabled. In both the cases, we skip recording statistics.

Next, we update the table with session data. We change the number of hits, session end time, and exit page. The number of hits is a special case. All other fields will be made database-safe by TYPO3 automatically. The number of hits need not be escaped because we will simply increment it. This way, we avoid the SQL SELECT query to fetch the number of hits. Very small but important performance improvement!

Next, we execute a query to update page statistics. At this moment, the statistics record for the current page may not yet exist in the database. We detect this case by examining the number of updated rows and inserting a record if necessary. This is again a small optimization in the code.

Finally, if a new record was inserted, we update the reference index for this record.

Here is the implementation:

```
function updateSession() {
    // Get session data
    $session_data = $GLOBALS['TSFE']->fe_user->getKey('ses',
        self::SESSION_KEY);
    if (is_array($session_data)) {
        // Update session hit counter and length
        $fields = array(
            'session_end' => $GLOBALS['SIM_EXEC_TIME'],
            'last_page' => $GLOBALS['TSFE']->id,
            'hits' => 'hits+1'
        );
        $GLOBALS['TYPO3_DB']->exec_UPDATEquery(
            'tx_feuserstat_sessions',
            'uid=' . intval($session_data['session_uid']),
```

```
        $fields, array('hits'));
    // Update current page stats
    // (or insert new page stat record)
    $fields = array(
        'hits' => 'hits+1',
    );
    $GLOBALS['TYPO3_DB']->exec_UPDATEquery(
        'tx_feuserstat_pagestats',
        'sesstat_uid=' . intval(
            $session_data['session_uid']) .
        ' AND page_uid=' . $GLOBALS['TSFE']->id,
        $fields, array('hits'));
    if ($GLOBALS['TYPO3_DB']->sql_affected_rows() == 0) {
        // First visit to this page
        $fields = array(
            'pid' => intval($session_data['pid']),
            'fe_user' => intval(
                $GLOBALS['TSFE']->fe_user->user['uid']),
            'page_uid' => $GLOBALS['TSFE']->id,
            'sesstat_uid' => intval(
                $session_data['session_uid']),
        );
        $GLOBALS['TYPO3_DB']->exec_INSERTquery(
            'tx_feuserstat_pagestats', $fields);
        $ref = t3lib_div::makeInstance('t3lib_refindex');
        /* @var $ref t3lib_refindex */
        $ref->updateRefIndexTable(
            'tx_feuserstat_pagestats',
            $GLOBALS['TYPO3_DB']->sql_insert_id());
    }
  }
}
```

There are two points in the code that should catch the reader's attention. First, note how we specify the fields that should not be escaped automatically by TYPO3. The last argument for the $GLOBALS['TYPO3_DB']->exec_UPDATEquery is an array of such fields.

Another point is that we always sanitize the (intval) fields that we pass to the SQL query, even these are our own parameters (or at least, they are supposed to be ours). It may seem a little paranoid but when it comes to security, there is no excuse for giving any chance to an attacker to exploit your code.

To make the page statistics updates faster, we can add the following index to the `tx_feuserstat_pagestats` table:

```
KEY fe_update (sesstat_uid,page_uid)
```

You may remember from the previous chapters that keys should include several fields that participate in the query, and fields should be in the order they appear in the query.

Some readers may ask why we don't use a TYPO3 session ID, but create our own. It is true that TYPO3 has its own sessions for Frontend users. But these sessions leave as long as a user is logged in. If we refer to those sessions, we will have lots of meaningless numbers for session IDs in our tables. Instead, we use our own reference, which is persistent in the database.

This completes our implementation of the Frontend part.

Backend Modules: The Basics

In this section, we will briefly discuss the parts of a Backend module, the files it includes, and the API Backend modules it uses. This part is a necessary read if you are serious about Backend programming.

What Is a Backend Module?

A backend module is a piece of code that implements certain functionality in TYPO3 Backend and presents it on the screen.

Some modules can integrate them inside other modules. For example, the RealURL extension integrates itself into the **Web | Info** module. Kickstarter integrates itself into the Extension Manager. Integration usually creates a new function in the module.

Module Functions

Backend modules may either have one function or provide several functions. When a module provides several functions, they are usually shown as a select box in the module. This is known as a *module menu*. TYPO3 has an API for handling such menus. It can store the menu number for a module. When a user comes back to the module, they will see the same menu item where they were when they left. Also, a module can store data with the menu and merge user submitted data with the module's already saved data. All these API services help to create modules with session persistence. We will see corresponding functions later in this section.

The following screenshot shows the module menu in the Extension Manager:

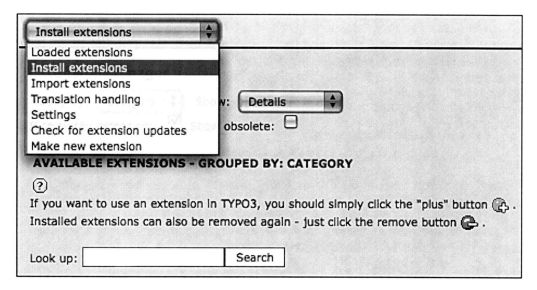

Backend Module Files

Each Backend module is located inside its own directory inside the extension. Traditionally, modules are located in the directories prefixed with mod.

TYPO3 requires only one file for each module. The file is named conf.php. It contains all information about the module. Here is an example of conf.php from our extension, as generated by the Kickstarter (this may change after the book is printed!):

```php
<?php
    // DO NOT REMOVE OR CHANGE THESE 3 LINES:
define('TYPO3_MOD_PATH', '../typo3conf/ext/feuserstat/mod1/');
$BACK_PATH='../../../../typo3/';
$MCONF['name']='web_txfeuserstatM1';

$MCONF['access']='user,group';
$MCONF['script']='index.php';
$MLANG['default']['tabs_images']['tab'] = 'moduleicon.gif';
$MLANG['default']['ll_ref']=
            'LLL:EXT:feuserstat/mod1/locallang_mod.xml';
?>
```

The first three code lines are modified by TYPO3 as necessary. The first two are not very interesting for us. The third tells our module name as known internally to TYPO3.

This line contains the internal module name. The internal module name consists of a parent module name, underscore character, and generated module identifier, which in turn consists of tx, extension key, M, and the module number in the extension. If a module is to be moved to another parent module, the first parent (before the underscore character) must be adjusted. Such a change actually moves submodules between modules.

The next code line defines who can access the module. Possible values are:

- admin for admin-only access
- user, group for making access to user and group

$MCONF['script'] defines which file will be executed as a module. Normally, it is index.php.

The $MLANG['default']['tabs_images']['tab'] defines module icon. The file name is typically left as it is, but the icon is changed.

The last line, $MLANG['default']['ll_ref'], defines a file with language labels for the module.

The conf.php file is rarely changed. If changes happen, typically, the access mode is adjusted, or the module is moved to another parent module.

Backend API

Backend modules can freely use most of the classes in the t3lib/ directory. We will review some most used classes here.

t3lib_BEfunc

t3lib_BEfunc is a collection of functions for Backend. We already know about t3lib_div, which provides many convenient functions. t3lib_BEfunc is similar, but limited to Backend.

The most important functions in this class are deleteClause and BEenableFields. Together, they provide an equivalent of $this->cObj->enableFields in Frontend.

Another useful function is readPageAccess. It accepts the page uid value and the permission clause (typically provided by $GLOBALS['BE_USER']->getPagePermsClause(1)). If this function returns false, it means the current user does not have access to the page. Otherwise, the function returns the page record.

`BEgetRootLine` is a rough equivalent of Frontend functions to retrieve the rootline. It is not the exact re-implementation of the Frontend. `BEgetRootLine` will stop only when it reaches a page record with `pid` field set to zero. The equivalent Frontend function will return a root line up to the root of the website.

`cshItem` allows us to create context sensitive help (CSH) for table records. It accepts the table name, field name, and a module's `BACK_PATH`. It will return a linked help icon. When hovered or clicked, the icon will present a help for the field in the table (if defined).

`getModTSconfig` retrieves TSConfig for the module by page id and path. We will see how this function works later in this chapter.

`getModuleData` is a very useful function if a programmer wants to store certain data for the module. Information is Backend user dependent. This function accepts three parameters: an array of default values, an array of current values, and module name. The result is default data overridden by the already saved data and overridden yet more by the changed settings. This result is also saved to the current user record. Thus, persistence for the module can be maintained.

`getRecord` retrieves a record from the table by its ID. It is simply a convenient method. There is a companion function named `getRecordRaw`, which accepts the table name and SQL `WHERE` condition.

`getRecordTitle` will return a title of the record as shown by the **List** module.

t3lib_TCEmain

This class is one of the most important classes in TYPO3. It processes absolutely all record creation, modification, removal, and versioning in the TYPO3 Backend (excluding most extensions). This class can and must be used by extensions. There are several reasons to use this class instead of direct database access:

- It takes into account several factors to create data properly
- It maintains links between records
- It checks permissions
- It records data in proper formats (including many-to-many database relations)
- It calls hooks from other extensions

The most important functions include `clear_cacheCmd`, `process_cmdmap`, and `process_datamap`.

`clear_cacheCmd` will clear cache for the given argument. `all` will clear all `cache_` tables. `pages` will clear page cache. `temp_CACHED` will clear cache files. An integer value will clear a page with this id. The first three commands are available only to the admin user or to the user who has corresponding `option.clearCache` in the User TSConfig. The last (integer) value can also be used from the Frontend, though this is not documented.

`process_datamap` works with a data array supplied to the `start` class function. It accepts an array with keys equal to table names. Each value is also an array where the key is either an ID or a string starting with `NEW` and value is a record array. The following is an example of creating a new record in the `tx_myext_table` table:

```
$data = array(
    'tx_myext_table' => array(
        uniqid('NEW') => array(
            'pid' => $pid,
            'crdate' => time(),
            ...
        ),
    ),
);
$tce = t3lib_div::makeInstance('t3lib_TCEmain');
/* @var $tce t3lib_TCEmain */
$tce->start($data, null),
$tce->process_datamap();
if (count($tce->errorLog)) {
    // Process errors here
}
```

This is all a programmer needs to create a new record in the database!

It is possible to create, for example, pages and content elements on these pages at the same time. In this case, `pid` must have the corresponding `NEW` value.

`process_cmdmap` works in a similar way. The format is a little different. The table name and ID are still present (no `NEW` value though), but they point to a command array specific to each command. Command examples are `move`, `copy`, `version`, `delete`, and so on. The data array depends on the command. The format of the data is different for each command. The best way to find the information is to look through the source code.

t3lib_TCEforms

This class shows all Backend forms. It can be used from extensions as well. The example of using TCEform exists in the TYPO3 core. The workspaces module (`typo3/mod/user/ws`) contains a customized TCEform for `sys_workspaces`.

t3lib_htmlmail

This class allows us to send HTML and plain emails with attachments. There is an explanation for usage in the beginning of the class. Here, we provide a simple code example:

```
$mail = t3lib_div::makeInstance('t3lib_htmlmail');
/* @var $mail t3lib_htmlmail */
$mail->start();
$mail->useQuotedPrintable();
$mail->returnPath = $mail->from_email = $mail->replyto_email =
    $mail->from_name = $mail->replyto_name =
        $sender;
$mail->recipient = '"' . addslashes($recipient_name) .
    '" <' . $recipient_email . '>';
$mail->subject = $subject;
$mail->addPlain($message);
// Attachments
for ($i = 0; $i < count($attachments); $i++) {
    $mail->addAttachment($attachments[$i]);
}
$result = $mail->send('');
```

t3lib_refindex

This is a reference index processing class, which we have already seen when we programmed a Frontend plugin.

$BE_USER

This is a global instance of the t3lib_beUserAuth class. It is similar to the Frontend user (shares the same base classes). The user record is available through the user attribute (array). There is also a boolean admin property, which is set to true if the user is an admin.

Implementing a Backend Module

In this section, we will implement the Backend module of our extension. Our Backend module will not use many functions, but the reader can extend it as required to include additional functionality.

Files and Classes

Our Backend module is going to be large. Therefore, we will have a main class for making the menu and dispatching code to other included files. The other files will have classes for showing:

- The fixed number of logins
- The Monthly view
- The Active and inactive views (the same class)
- The Page hit statistics for each user and optionally, the session

Classes and files will appear as follows:

File name	Class name
index.php	tx_geuserstat_module1
class.tx_feuserstat_logins.php	tx_feuserstat_logins
class.tx_feuserstat_monthly.php	tx_feuserstat_monthly
class.tx_feuserstat_active.php	tx_feuserstat_active
class.tx_feuserstat_pagestats.php	tx_feuserstat_pagestats

All files will be there in the mod1 subdirectory. Each class will have a main method. It will accept a pointer to a calling class ($pObj parameter). In the case of tx_feuserstat_active, it is a boolean parameter saying whether we show active or inactive users.

A Note about Backend HTML

At the moment of writing this book, Backend modules did not have a good equivalent of Frontend templating. Some functions existing in t3lib_parsehtml can be used for templating, but mostly HTML is hard-coded in Backend modules.

Backend modules use a document to generate output. A document is an attempt to hide the lack of templating and styling for Backend behind several methods and variables.

There are several types of documents (smallDoc, mediumDoc, largeDoc, and noDoc). They differ on the width of the output area. noDoc does not limit the width.

A document is created and initialized inside the generated `main` method in the following way:

```
$this->doc = t3lib_div::makeInstance('mediumDoc');
$this->doc->backPath = $GLOBALS['BACK_PATH'];
$this->content .= $this->doc->startPage(
        $GLOBALS['LANG']->getLL('title'));
$this->content.=$this->doc->header(
        $GLOBALS['LANG']->getLL('title'));
$this->content.=$this->doc->spacer(15);
```

The code above creates an instance of mediumDoc. Next, a path to this module is set to the document instance. This is necessary to generate links correctly inside the document.

The line with the `startPage` call generates markup to start the page. This includes page title and form tag. The whole module output will be enclosed to the form and ready for submission.

The line with the `header` call creates a header. Using the `header` function to create headers makes all modules in the system look similar.

The last line creates a vertical spacer on the page.

Implementing the Main Class

According to the table above, the main class of the module is located in `mod1/index.php`. There is nothing much to modify there. Mostly, `global` declaration should be removed, and the global variables should be changed accordingly to use `$GLOBAL`. The only method that needs changes to implement module functionality is `moduleContent`. This method dispatches calls to other classes. The output of the classes is wrapped into a "section" (a part of "Document" we discussed earlier).

Here is the code:

```
    protected function moduleContent() {
        $function = intval($this->MOD_SETTINGS['function']);
        switch ($function) {
            case 1:
                $mod = t3lib_div::makeInstance(
                    'tx_feuserstat_logins');
                /* @var $mod tx_fe_userstat_active */
                $this->content .= $this->doc->section(
                    $GLOBALS['LANG']->getLL('last_logins'),
                    $mod->main($this), 0, 1);
                break;
```

```
    case 2:
        $mod = t3lib_div::makeInstance(
            'tx_feuserstat_monthly');
        /* @var $mod tx_fe_userstat_active */
        $this->content .= $this->doc->section(
            $GLOBALS['LANG']->getLL('monthly_view'),
            $mod->main($this), 0, 1);
        break;
    case 3:
        $mod = t3lib_div::makeInstance(
            'tx_feuserstat_active');
        /* @var $mod tx_fe_userstat_active */
        $this->content .= $this->doc->section(
            $GLOBALS['LANG']->getLL('active_log'),
            $mod->main($this, true), 0, 1);
        break;
    case 4:
        $mod = t3lib_div::makeInstance(
            'tx_feuserstat_active');
        /* @var $mod tx_fe_userstat_active */
        $this->content .= $this->doc->section(
            $GLOBALS['LANG']->getLL('inactive_log'),
            $mod->main($this, false), 0, 1);
        break;
    }
}
```

Implementing the List of Last Logins

The list of last logins is in the tx_feuserstat_logins class. We select a fixed amount of maximum 200 users from tx_feuserstat_sessions and sort them by session_start. The reader can, for an exercise, implement a configurable number of users either as a TSConfig option, or as a form in the Backend module. The TSConfig example will be shown later in this chapter. In the case of the form, do not forget to pass the id parameter to the index.php.

Here is how the list of the last logins looks:

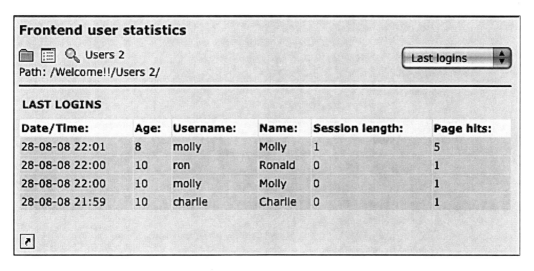

After selecting the rows, we will generate HTML for each row and collect it in the array. After collecting all rows, we implode the array and wrap it with `table` tags. This technique is commonly used in the TYPO3 core for repeating activities.

Here is the implementation of the function:

```
public function main(&$pObj) {
    $userId = intval(t3lib_div::GPvar('useruid'));
    $sessId = intval(t3lib_div::_GP('sessid'));
    $list = array();
    // TODO Configurable limit!
    $query = 'SELECT t1.*,t2.username,t2.name,t2.uid AS ' .
    'user_uid FROM ' .
        'tx_feuserstat_sessions t1,fe_users t2 WHERE ' .
        't2.uid=t1.fe_user'.
        ($userId ? ' AND t2.uid='.intval($userId) : '').
        ($sessId ? ' AND t1.uid=' . $sessId : '') .
        ' AND t2.pid = '.intval($pObj->id).
        t3lib_BEfunc::deleteClause('fe_users', 't2').
        ' ORDER BY session_start DESC LIMIT 200';
    $res = $GLOBALS['TYPO3_DB']->sql_query($query);
    while (($row = $GLOBALS['TYPO3_DB']->sql_fetch_assoc(
            $res))) {
        $extra = '';
        if ($userId) {
            $extra .= '&sessid=' . $row['uid'];
```

```
        }
        $list[] = '<tr bgcolor="' . $pObj->doc->bgColor4 . '">
            <td nowrap>' .
            date($GLOBALS['TYPO3_CONF_VARS']['SYS']['ddmmyy'] .
            ' ' . $GLOBALS['TYPO3_CONF_VARS']['SYS']['hhmm'],
$row['session_start']) . '</td>
            <td nowrap>' . t3lib_BEfunc::calcAge(time() -
                $row['session_start'],
            $GLOBALS['LANG']->getLL('minutesHoursDaysYears')) .
            '</td>
            <td nowrap><a href="index.php?id=' . $pObj->id .
            '&useruid=' . $row['user_uid'].$extra.'">' .
            $row['username'].'</a></td>
            <td nowrap>' . $row['name'].'</td>
            <td nowrap>' .
            t3lib_BEfunc::calcAge($row['session_end'] -
            $row['session_start'],
            $GLOBALS['LANG']->getLL('minutesHoursDaysYears')) .
            '</td>
            <td>' . $row['hits'] . '</td>
            </tr>
        ';
    }
    $GLOBALS['TYPO3_DB']->sql_free_result($res);
    $content = '<table border="0" cellpadding="1"
        cellspacing="1" width="100%">
        <tr bgcolor="' . $pObj->doc->bgColor5 . '">
        <td><strong>' .
        $GLOBALS['LANG']->getLL('header_datetime') .
        '</strong></td>
        <td><strong>' .
        $GLOBALS['LANG']->getLL('header_age') .
        '</strong></td>
        <td><strong>' .
        $GLOBALS['LANG']->getLL('header_username') .
        '</strong></td>
        <td><strong>' .
        $GLOBALS['LANG']->getLL('header_name') .
        '</strong></td>
        <td><strong>' .
        $GLOBALS['LANG']->getLL('header_session_lgd') .
        '</strong></td>
        <td><strong>' .
        $GLOBALS['LANG']->getLL('header_pagehits') .
```

```
                '</strong></td>
                </tr>
                ' . implode('', $list) . '</table>';
            if ($userId > 0) {
                $inst = t3lib_div::makeInstance(
                    'tx_feuserstat_pagestats');
                /* @var $inst tx_feuserstat_pagestats */
                $content = '<a href="index.php?id=' . $pObj->id .
                    ($sessId ? '&useruid=' . $userId : '') .
                    '"><strong>' . $GLOBALS['LANG']->getLL($sessId ?
                    'modulecont_listAllSessions' :
                    'modulecont_listAllUsers') .
                    '</strong></a><br /> <br />' . $content .
                    $pObj->doc->section(
                        $GLOBALS['LANG']->getLL('header_pagestats'),
                        $sessId ?
                            $inst->getPageStatsForSession($pObj->doc,
                                $sessId) :
                            $inst->getPageStats($pObj->doc, $userId)) .
                    '<br /> <br />';
            }
            return $content;
        }
```

This code also demonstrates the usage of the `$GLOBALS['TYPO3_DB']->sql_query()` function. This function can be used to execute complex queries directly. It is especially useful when a query contains constructions that cannot be understood by other TYPO3 functions. Such constructions include (but are not limited to) UNION and JOIN.

Furthermore, we can also see the usage of `$GLOBALS['TYPO3_CONF_VARS']['SYS']['ddmmyy']` and `$GLOBALS['TYPO3_CONF_VARS']['SYS']['ddmmyy']`. These two system settings contain date and time formats. Mostly, they are used in Backend. Frontend may have its own settings to accommodate a designer's requirements better. But the Backend modules should use these settings for consistency with other Backend modules.

Implementing Monthly View

Monthly view shows login statistics by the month. For each user, it displays how many times a user logged into the Frontend. Sorting goes from most visits to least visits. Here is how this view looks:

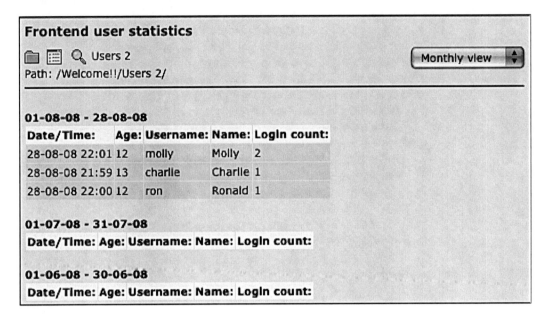

The code follows:

```
function main(&$pObj) {
    $userId = intval(t3lib_div::GPvar('useruid'));
    $times = array();
    $times[0] = time();
    for ($a = 1; $a <= 12; $a++) {
        $times[$a] = mktime(0, 0, 0, date('m') + 1 - $a, 1);
    }
    $content = '';
    for ($a = 0; $a < 12; $a++) {
        $list = array();
        $query = 'SELECT t1.*,t2.username,t2.name,t2.uid ' .
          'AS user_uid, count(*) AS counter, ' .
               'MAX(session_start) AS last_login FROM ' .
               'tx_feuserstat_sessions t1, fe_users t2 ' .
               'WHERE t2.uid=t1.fe_user' .
          ($userId > 0 ? ' AND t2.uid=' .
          intval($userId) : '') .
          ' AND t2.pid = ' . intval($pObj->id).
```

```
                ' AND t1.session_start<' . intval($times[$a]) .
                ' AND t1.session_start>=' .
                intval($times[$a+1]).
                t3lib_BEfunc::deleteClause('fe_users', 't2') .
                ' GROUP BY t2.uid ORDER BY counter DESC ' .
                'LIMIT 200';
    $res = $GLOBALS['TYPO3_DB']->sql_query($query);
    while (($row = $GLOBALS['TYPO3_DB']->sql_fetch_assoc(
            $res))) {
        $list[] = '<tr bgcolor="' . $pObj->doc->bgColor4 .
            '"><td nowrap>' . date(
            $GLOBALS['TYPO3_CONF_VARS']['SYS']['ddmmyy']
            . ' ' .
            $GLOBALS['TYPO3_CONF_VARS']['SYS']['hhmm'],
            $row['last_login']) . '</td>
            <td nowrap="nowrap">' .
            t3lib_BEfunc::calcAge(time() -
            $row['session_end'],
            $GLOBALS['LANG']->getLL(
            'minutesHoursDaysYears')) . '</td>
            <td nowrap><a href="index.php?id=' .
            $pObj->id . '&useruid=' . $row['user_uid'] .
            '">' . $row['username'] . '</a></td>
            <td nowrap>' . $row['name'] . '</td>
            <td>' . $row['counter'] . '</td>
            </tr>
            ';
    }
    $GLOBALS['TYPO3_DB']->sql_free_result($res);
    $content .= '<br />' .
    $GLOBALS['LANG']->getLL('period') .
    '<strong>' .
    date($GLOBALS['TYPO3_CONF_VARS']['SYS']['ddmmyy'],
    $times[$a+1]) . ' - ' .
    date($GLOBALS['TYPO3_CONF_VARS']['SYS']['ddmmyy'],
    $times[$a] - 1) . '</strong><br />
    <table border="0" cellpadding="1" cellspacing="1">
    <tr bgColor="' . $pObj->doc->bgColor5 . '">
    <td><strong>' .
    $GLOBALS['LANG']->getLL('header_datetime') .
    '</strong></td><td><strong>' .
    $GLOBALS['LANG']->getLL('header_age').'</strong></td>
    <td><strong>' .
    $GLOBALS['LANG']->getLL('header_username') .
```

```
            '</strong></td><td><strong>' .
        $GLOBALS['LANG']->getLL('header_name') .
            '</strong></td><td><strong>' .
        $GLOBALS['LANG']->getLL('header_logins') .
            '</strong></td></tr>
            ' . implode('', $list) . '</table>';
    }
    if ($userId > 0) {
        $content = '<a href="index.php?id=' . $pObj->id .
            '"><strong>' .
            $GLOBALS['LANG']->getLL('modulecont_listAllUsers')
            . '</strong></a><br>' . $content;
    }
    return $content;
}
```

Now, we already have two functions in the module!

Implementing a List of Active Users

The list of active users shows the recently logged in users. We will show a maximum of 200 users for a period of the last 90 days. These limits can be changed by making a form in the module to enter these values or by using page TSConfig for new defaults. A TSConfig example is shown in the code. The reader is encouraged to implement the alternative form as an exercise.

Here is the screenshot of this view:

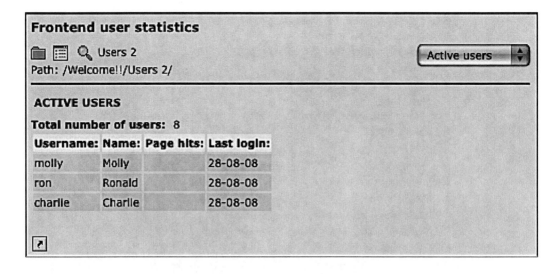

Chapter 7

To change the number of days through TSConfig, a user can enter the following property in the page TSConfig on the page where the user records are stored:

```
mod.web_txfeuserstatM1.activeLogins.days = 120
```

In this example, we change the number of days from the default of 90 to 120.

The code of the function follows:

```
function main(&$pObj, $showActive) {
    // Get number of days from module TSConfig
    $tsConfig = t3lib_BEfunc::getModTSconfig($pObj->id,
            'mod.' . $GLOBALS['MCONF']['name'] .
            '.activeLogins.days');
    $daysBack = t3lib_div::testInt($tsConfig['value']) ?
            intval($tsConfig['value']) : 90;
        // Total number of users:
    list($row) = $GLOBALS['TYPO3_DB']->exec_SELECTgetRows(
            'COUNT(*) AS t',
            'fe_users',
            'pid=' . intval($pObj->id) .
            t3lib_BEfunc::deleteClause('fe_users'));
    $content.= '<strong>' .
            $GLOBALS['LANG']->getLL('total_number_of_users') .
            '</strong> ' . $row['t'];
    $query = 'SELECT uid,username,email,name,lastlogin' .
        ' FROM fe_users'.
        ' WHERE pid=' . intval($pObj->id) .
        ' AND lastlogin ' . ($showActive ? '>=' : '<') .
        (time() - $daysBack*24*3600) .
        t3lib_BEfunc::deleteClause('fe_users') .
        ' ORDER BY lastlogin DESC LIMIT 200';
    $res = $GLOBALS['TYPO3_DB']->sql_query($query);
    $tableRows = array();
    $tableRows[] = '<tr bgcolor="' .
        $GLOBALS['TBE_TEMPLATE']->bgColor5 . '">
        <td nowrap><strong>' .
        $GLOBALS['LANG']->getLL('header_username') .
        '</strong></td>
        <td nowrap><strong>' .
        $GLOBALS['LANG']->getLL('header_name') .
        '</strong></td>
        <td nowrap><strong>' .
        $GLOBALS['LANG']->getLL('header_email') .
        '</strong></td><td nowrap><strong>' .
```

```
                $GLOBALS['LANG']->getLL('header_lastlogin') .
                '</strong></td></tr>';
        while (($row = $GLOBALS['TYPO3_DB']->sql_fetch_assoc(
                $res))) {
            $tableRows[] = '<tr bgcolor="' .
                $GLOBALS['TBE_TEMPLATE']->bgColor4 . '">
                <td nowrap>' . htmlspecialchars($row['username']) .
                '</td><td nowrap>' .
                htmlspecialchars($row['name']) .
                '</td><td nowrap>' .
                htmlspecialchars($row['email']) .
                '</td><td nowrap>' .
                htmlspecialchars(date(
                    $GLOBALS['TYPO3_CONF_VARS']['SYS']['ddmmyy'],
                    $row['lastlogin'])) .
                '</td></tr>';
        }
        $content .= '<table border="0" cellpadding="1" ' .
            'cellspacing="2">' .
            implode('', $tableRows) . '</table>';
        $GLOBALS['TYPO3_DB']->sql_free_result($res);
        return $content;
    }
```

As seen from the code, we use the t3lib_BEfunc::getModTSconfig function to obtain module TSConfig. This function accepts two arguments:

- page id
  This is the ID of the page to fetch TSConfig for. Different pages can have different TSConfigs.

- TSConfig path
  This is the path to TSConfig that we want to examine. It is a list of TSConfig properties separated by a dot. In our case, we use mod.web_ txfeuserstatM1.activeLogins.days.

As usual with TypoScript, the same property can have a value and point to an array of subproperties. The t3lib_BEfunc::getModTSconfig function will return an array consisting of two keys:

- value
  This key points to a single value of the TSConfig property found at the given path. If no value is found, it will be null.

- properties
  An array of properties or array (with dot appended) of deeper TSConfig levels.

In our case, we just query the value directly. If the reader adds another property (for example, userLimit), they would query TSConfig differently:

```
$tsConfig = t3lib_BEfunc::getModTSconfig($pObj->id,
        'mod.' . $GLOBALS['MCONF']['name'] . '.activeLogins');
$daysBack = $tsConfig['properties']['days'];
$userLimit = $tsConfig['properties']['userLimit'];
```

TSConfig is often a good way to customize module appearance or functionality. When implementing the real module in your extension, think what you want to leave to TSConfig, and what you want to put into the form inside the module. Many settings are easily changeable by users and should be in the form instead of TSConfig.

Implementing Page Statistics

Page statistics use SQL LEFT JOIN to show the page information for the user or user session. The page may be removed or be inaccessible to the current user. Therefore, we have to take care to show the statistics while not showing the page title or a link to it. This is important from both completeness and security point of views.

Since there can be a lot of pages, our example uses the hard-coded number of pages to show (64). The reader can make this value configurable as an exercise.

The code is longer than in the previous cases:

```
function getPageStatsForSession(&$doc, $session_id) {
    /* @var $doc mediumDoc */
    $content = '<table width="100%" border="0"
        cellpadding="1" cellspacing="1">' .
        '<tr bgcolor="' . $doc->bgColor5 . '">' .
        '<td><strong>' .
        $GLOBALS['LANG']->getLL('header_pid') .
        '</strong></td><td><strong>' .
        $GLOBALS['LANG']->getLL('header_pagetitle') .
        '</strong></td><td><strong>' .
        $GLOBALS['LANG']->getLL('header_pagehits') .
        '</strong></td><td><strong>' .
        $GLOBALS['LANG']->getLL('header_firsthit') .
        '</strong></td><td><strong>' .
        $GLOBALS['LANG']->getLL('header_lasthit') .
        '</strong></td></tr>';
    // Get records
    $res = $GLOBALS['TYPO3_DB']->sql_query(
        'SELECT t1.page_uid,t2.title,t1.hits,t1.crdate, ' .
        ' t1.tstamp FROM tx_feuserstat_pagestats t1 ' .
```

```
            'LEFT JOIN pages t2 ON ' .
            't1.page_uid=t2.uid WHERE sesstat_uid=' .
            intval($session_id) .
            t3lib_BEfunc::deleteClause('pages', 't2') .
            str_replace('pages.', 't2.',
                t3lib_BEfunc::BEenableFields('pages')) .
            ' ORDER BY t1.hits DESC');
    $num = 0;
    $numResults = $GLOBALS['TYPO3_DB']->sql_num_rows($res);
    while ($num < 64 &&
            false != ($ar =
            $GLOBALS['TYPO3_DB']->sql_fetch_assoc($res))) {
        $content .= '<tr bgcolor="' . $doc->bgColor4 .
            '"><td>' .
            $ar['page_uid'] . '</td><td>' .
            '<a target="_blank" href="' .
            t3lib_div::getIndpEnv('TYPO3_REQUEST_HOST') .
            '/index.php?id=' . $ar['page_uid'] . '">' .
            htmlspecialchars($ar['title']) . '</a></td><td>' .
            $ar['hits'] . '</td><td>' .
            date(
                $GLOBALS['TYPO3_CONF_VARS']['SYS']['ddmmyy'] .
                ' ' .
                $GLOBALS['TYPO3_CONF_VARS']['SYS']['hhmm'],
                $ar['crdate']) .
            '</td><td>' .
            date(
                $GLOBALS['TYPO3_CONF_VARS']['SYS']['ddmmyy'] .
                ' ' .
                $GLOBALS['TYPO3_CONF_VARS']['SYS']['hhmm'],
                $ar['tstamp']) .
            '</td></tr>';
        $num++;
    }
    $GLOBALS['TYPO3_DB']->sql_free_result($res);
    if ($num < $numResults) {
        $content .= '<tr><td colspan="4">' . sprintf(
            $GLOBALS['LANG']->getLL('message_moreresults'),
            $numResults - $num) .
            '</td></tr>';
    }
    $content .= '</table>';
    return $content;
}
```

```
/**
 * Makes report about visited pages.
 *
 * @param    mediumDoc    $doc   Document (like mediumDoc)
 * @param    int    $user  User ID
 * @return    string Generated HTML
 */
function getPageStats(&$doc, $user) {
    /* @var $doc mediumDoc */
    $content = '<table width="100%" border="0"
        cellpadding="1" cellspacing="1">' .
        '<tr bgcolor="' . $doc->bgColor5 . '">' .
        '<td><strong>' .
        $GLOBALS['LANG']->getLL('header_pid') .
        '</strong></td><td><strong>' .
        $GLOBALS['LANG']->getLL('header_pagetitle') .
        '</strong></td><td><strong>' .
        $GLOBALS['LANG']->getLL('header_numsessions') .
        '</strong></td><td><strong>' .
        $GLOBALS['LANG']->getLL('header_pagehits') .
        '</strong></td><td><strong>' .
        $GLOBALS['LANG']->getLL('header_firsthit') .
        '</strong></td><td><strong>' .
        $GLOBALS['LANG']->getLL('header_lasthit') .
        '</strong></td></tr>';
    // Get records
    $res = $GLOBALS['TYPO3_DB']->sql_query(
            'SELECT COUNT(page_uid) AS num_sessions, ' .
            'SUM(hits) AS num_hits, ' .
            'MIN(t1.crdate) AS crdate, MAX(t1.tstamp) AS ' .
            'tstamp, page_uid, title FROM ' .
            'tx_feuserstat_pagestats t1 LEFT JOIN pages t2 ' .
            'ON t1.page_uid=t2.uid WHERE fe_user=' .
             intval($user) .
            t3lib_BEfunc::deleteClause('pages', 't2') .
            ' GROUP BY page_uid ORDER BY hits DESC'
        );
    $num = 0;
    $numResults = $GLOBALS['TYPO3_DB']->sql_num_rows($res);
    while ($num < 64 && false != ($ar =
            $GLOBALS['TYPO3_DB']->sql_fetch_assoc($res))) {
        $content .= '<tr bgcolor="' . $doc->bgColor4 .
            '"><td>' . $ar['page_uid'] . '</td><td>' .
            '<a target="_blank" href="' .
```

```
        t3lib_div::getIndpEnv('TYPO3_REQUEST_HOST') .
        '/index.php?id=' . $ar['page_uid'] . '">' .
        htmlspecialchars($ar['title']) . '</a></td><td>' .
        $ar['num_sessions'] . '</td><td>' .
        $ar['num_hits'] . '</td><td>' .
        date(
            $GLOBALS['TYPO3_CONF_VARS']['SYS']['ddmmyy'] .
            ' ' .
            $GLOBALS['TYPO3_CONF_VARS']['SYS']['hhmm'],
            $ar['crdate']) .
        '</td><td>' .
        date(
            $GLOBALS['TYPO3_CONF_VARS']['SYS']['ddmmyy'] .
            ' ' .
            $GLOBALS['TYPO3_CONF_VARS']['SYS']['hhmm'],
            $ar['tstamp']) .
        '</td></tr>';
    $num++;
}
$GLOBALS['TYPO3_DB']->sql_free_result($res);
if ($num < $numResults) {
    $content .= '<tr><td colspan="4">' . sprintf(
        $GLOBALS['LANG']->getLL('message_moreresults'),
        $numResults - $num) .
        '</td></tr>';
}
$content .= '</table>';
return $content;
}
```

The phpDoc comments are removed from the code to save space. Actual code should always have phpDoc comments.

The code also informs a user if there are more results as shown. We use `sprintf` to format results in a localization friendly way.

Summary

In this chapter, we learned the Backend module theory and programmed our own Backend module. The reader should now be able to make his own Backend modules.

8

Finalizing Extensions

In this chapter, we will prepare our extension for external use. This involves several steps that make an extension look better and more convenient for users. After completing these steps, an extension can be sent to the TYPO3 extension repository (TER).

Overview

When extension programming is completed, there should be additional steps taken before an extension is published. These steps add significant value to the quality of the extension. The steps include:

- Updating code files
  This involves checking the code once again for possible problems and missing code lines. Additionally, the function index should be created for each code file.

- Writing documentation
  This involves creating manuals for the extension.

Updating Code Files

Updating code files makes sure that an extension code is free from obvious errors.

Checking the Code

The first thing to do is to check your code again. Some things may have been missed during development, and now it is time to recover them. Use the following checklist to check your code.

- Are all the `require_once` statements in place?
  It is easy to forget some of these statements during development if you are logged into TYPO3 Backend and running Frontend code. The code will work, but it will fail when running standalone.

- Are all the request parameters checked?
  It is not enough to assign a variable from a request parameter and assume that it is always in the correct format. Check it and substitute it with a good default, or show an error message if defaults are not possible. The same goes for TypoScript setup.

- Are all SQL parameters sanitized?
  SQL injection is the most common problem for beginner PHP programmers and sometimes even for experienced programmers. Always use the `fullQuoteStr` or `intval` for SQL parameters.

- Do all `case` statements have `break` statements or `Fall through` comments?
  If there is no `break` statement for a `case` statement, then it is an unintentional error or an intentional deletion. If it is an intentional deletion, write a comment about it!

- Do XCLASS declarations exist in every code file?
  XCLASS declarations must be there in every code file. It allows others to extend your classes without modifying them and losing the changes with an update.

- Are XCLASS declarations correct?
  First, check if the file names are correct in XCLASS declarations. Next, ensure that there are no extra spaces or missing spaces. Formatting is very important for XCLASS statements. Check the extension information screen in TYPO3 Extension Manager for missing XCLASS declarations. If the Extension Managers lists some, but you have an XCLASS declaration in that class, it means that the formatting is wrong.

- Are all extended tables mentioned in `ext_emconf.php`?
  All extended tables should be mentioned in the `modify_tables` option of `ext_emconf.php`.

- Do all functions have phpDoc blocks?
  If not, add these blocks. Read more about phpDoc on the phpDoc website at `http://www.phpdoc.org/`.

- Do functions have `public`/`protected`/`private` modifiers?
  If not, add them. Remember that `private` should be used with care as it prevents XCLASSing in some cases. It is better to use `protected` than `private`.

- Are there any empty lines at the end of PHP files?
  If yes, remove them, or they may break **gzip** encoding of Frontend output.

- Did you follow TYPO3 coding guidelines?
  Following coding guidelines is not a formality. They are developed in a way that helps to prevent certain typing and coding errors.

It is also good to scroll code slowly from top to bottom. This way, you can see flaws in the code, missing handlers, and obvious typos in parameter names. A review would help discover minor errors that your eyes may have missed when writing code.

Using extdeveval to Beautify your Code

Extension Development Evaluator (extdeveval) is a TYPO3 extension for developers to help them make their code better. It adds a new menu item to the `Tools` module in the TYPO3 Backend.

Developers will mostly be interested in several tools that extdeveval provides:

- PHP script documentation help – This will insert/reformat phpDoc in the file. Even if you are tempted to use this instead of writing comments manually, do not do this. You will still have to go and fill in stub comments generated by this function. But it is good for adding missing phpDoc parameters and verifying syntax in general.

- PHP source code tuning– This tool provides two options:
    ° Convert double quotes to single quotes (better PHP performance)
    ° Reformat/beautify PHP source code. This will format PHP code according to TYPO3 coding guidelines

- Calculator – This is not a mathematical calculator but a tool to convert SQL dates to Unix time stamps, create MD5 hashes out of pasted content, and create many more handy functions.

Let's see these functions in more detail.

Script Documentation

phpDoc comments in PHP files are important for several reasons.

First, they allow anyone (even the author after several months) to get an idea of the function's purpose. There can also be calling constraints, extra notes, and so on. Anything useful for the user of the function should go to phpDoc.

Next, phpDoc comments describe parameters. Parameters in TYPO3 functions can be very complex, and phpDoc helps to make a function more usable by providing information about parameter types and possible values.

phpDoc also describes the return type of a function. If a function does not return anything, use void as the return type.

Extdeveval will generate stub phpDoc comments where they are missing. It can recognize PHP type hinting and default attributes when necessary.

PHP script documentation function in extdeveval also adds a function index to the file. The next section discusses this in more detail.

Adding a Function Index

A function index helps to get a quick overview of the function list in the file. If the author uses a modern PHP IDE (such as Zend Studio or Komodo IDE) for PHP development, the function index may not seem important because IDEs can generate it on the fly in their GUI. However, the function index is helpful for people who use more generic tools for editing, or when a developer has to make adjustments to the code from the shell (for example, on the server outside of their usual development environment).

The function index is placed at the beginning of the file where the [CLASS/FUNCTION INDEX of SCRIPT] line is located. This line triggers creation of the function index. If it is missing, no index will be generated.

Here is an example of a function index as seen in t3lib/class.t3lib_db.php:

```
/**
 * [CLASS/FUNCTION INDEX of SCRIPT]
 *
 *
 *
 *   138: class t3lib_DB
 *
 *            SECTION: Query execution
 *   175:      function exec_INSERTquery($table,$fields_values,$no_
 *   192:      function exec_UPDATEquery($table,$where,$fields_valu
 *   206:      function exec_DELETEquery($table,$where)
 *   225:      function exec_SELECTquery($select_fields,$from_table
 *   250:      function exec_SELECT_mm_query($select,$local_table,$
 *   278:      function exec_SELECT_queryArray($queryParts)
 *   301:      function exec_SELECTgetRows($select_fields,$from_tab
```

The function index includes the line number and the full function declaration.

Reformatting the Code

Every TYPO3 extension should follow TYPO3 coding guidelines. This makes it easy for every developer to reuse the code or check it for problems.

Different people have different programming habits and different coding styles. There are over 3300 extensions available for TYPO3. It is hard to expect every author to follow the guidelines precisely. Here is where extdeveval comes into use.

Extdeveval can reformat the code according to TYPO3 coding guidelines. Developers select a file to reformat, and extdeveval does the rest. Usually, it is a safe operation, but it is a good idea to make a backup of the source file. Very seldom, extdeveval may corrupt the file.

This tool can also convert double quotes to single quotes. All TYPO3 code should use single quotes (with possible exception to `"\n"`). This saves some time for each request and may also prevent accidental variable expansion.

Writing Documentation (Extension Manual)

Good documentation is a very good reason for people to use an extension. An excellent extension without documentation will lose to an average extension with a good manual. The reason is simple – people use the extension manual to know what an extension does, how it looks and what it needs to run. In other words, it is like a manual for most home appliances: "no manual – hard to operate".

In this section, we will see how to write a good manual for a TYPO3 extension.

Documentation Template

TYPO3 requires extension manuals to follow the same format, and to be based on the same template. This requirement exists due to the TYPO3 Extension Repository (TER). TER renders manuals and makes them available online. All extension manuals are available at `http://typo3.org/documentation/document-library/extension-manuals/`. This is a very long page with a list of all available extension manuals.

A link to the manual is also available in the extension details at `typo3.org` website:

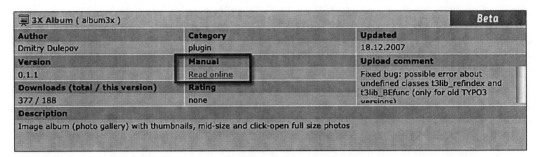

Manuals are created in the OpenOffice 1.0 format. The documentation template is available at `http://typo3.org/documentation/document-library/core-documentation/doc_template/current/`. To install the template, download it, open it in OpenOffice, and then save it as a template.

The saved template should be installed in OpenOffice. Open OpenOffice preferences (go to **Tools | Options**) and expand `OpenOffice` on the left. Then click on `Paths`. See where user the templates are located using `Template` entry on the right. There you will find the folder name where the saved template should be moved.

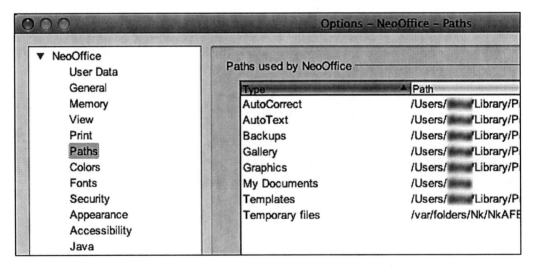

When starting a new manual, choose **File | New | Templates and Documents** in the OpenOffice. Navigate to **Templates**. Select TYPO3 documentation template there and a new document will be created. This document should be saved in the extension's `doc/` directory. The file must be saved in the OpenOffice 1.0 format (`sxw` file).

Template Structure

The template (and manual) has a certain structure, which should be followed in general. However, if the template section is not relevant to the extension, it should be removed. Do not leave empty sections in the manual! If you need it in the future, you can always add it back later.

The template starts from the title and the table of contents. Then comes the `Introduction` section. It contains the information that users read when they want to decide if an extension meets their requirements. This section also contains screenshots in the **Screenshots** section.

The next section is the **Users manual**. This part describes how to use an extension for the editor or the Frontend user.

The third section is for administrators and is present in the **Administration** section. It describes how to configure and administer an extension. This is for TYPO3 administrators.

The **Configuration** section describes how to configure an extension. It should list all TypoScript and Flexform properties.

The **Tutorial** section teaches one to use an extension in a quick and easy way (if possible).

The **Known problems** section shows the problems and limitations that the extension author recognizes.

The **To-Do list** section shows a list of tasks for the extension author. Of course, this section is optional.

The **ChangeLog** section is intended for listing changes in the extension. It does not really make sense to record changes in the manual because it makes manuals much longer, and no one really needs this information in the manual. The `ChangeLog` file in the extension's root directory is a much better place for it. The author of the book recommends leaving a single statement in this section: **See ChangeLog in the extension's directory**.

Styles in the Template

The documentation template has several predefined styles. These styles must be used in the documentation. Any other style will be ignored by the documentation renderer in the TYPO3 Extension Repository. The following styles are defined:

Style name	Usage
Text body	This is the default style to use for all normal text.
Table heading	This style is used to create table headings.
Table Contents	This style is used inside table cells that are not inside table headers.
Preformatted text	This style is used to create code examples, configuration examples, and so on.
Heading 1	This style is used for the main heading in the document. The documentation renderer will create a new HTML page for each of these headings.
Heading 2	This style is used for major text blocks inside Heading 1.
Heading 3	This style is used for separating text blocks further. Logically, it is a subheading.
Heading 4	This style is similar to heading 3, and is used for even deeper dividing texts.
Source text	This is a *character style*. It is used for inline code fragments.

These styles can be seen in OpenOffice's formatting toolbar.

Images in the Documentation

Images need special care in the TYPO3 manual. To render the documentation properly, images must be pasted as bitmaps to the document. This is accomplished by selecting **Edit** and then **Paste special** in the OpenOffice. There is a window where the documentation writer should select **Bitmap**. This will copy all image data to the document and allow the renderer to create an image on the server.

Writing Documentation

Writing a good documentation is not an easy task. There are lots of books for documentation writers on the Internet. The topic is large and cannot be covered here in full. However, we will try to provide certain advices. If the reader is interested in technical writing, he should consult special literature on this topic.

When starting a new manual, the first task is to update properties in the document. There are three properties: the standard property named `title` and two custom properties (`Email` and `Author`). Properties are accessed through the **File** menu, and a menu item named **Properties**.

Next, describe what the extension does. Try to avoid use of highly technical language wherever possible. This section is normally read by ordinary users to decide if they want use the extension and how.

Do not save on screenshots. Screenshots are important because they help users to understand what an extension's output or configuration looks like. At least one screenshot is required if your extension provides any output at all. It is good to mention that the extension's output is customizable by using a template.

When writing User and Administrator parts, do not assume that the reader knows the details as well as the writer does. It is okay to assume generic Unix shell or TYPO3 knowledge. However, all other instructions should be as detailed as possible. Knowledgeable users will just skip to the necessary parts. Beginners will be grateful for even the small details.

The configuration chapter needs a lot of attention. When writing in detail about configuration, follow the same style, type definitions, and example definitions as seen in the official TYPO3 documentation such as the TSRef of **TYPO3 Core API**.

It is important to give examples. Examples not only provide useful pieces of code, but also help people to understand the configuration better.

The quality of the example should be good. A trivial example should be followed by more complex examples.

The last but not the least part of the writing work is to update the table of contents (TOC) when finished with your writing. It is frustrating for users to navigate to a page mentioned in the TOC and find that the TOC is wrong. By the way, have you ever seen a book with a wrong TOC?

Making Documentation Available

If the documentation writer works on non-Windows systems, he/she may accidentally make the manual inaccessible. The problem happens when the user file permissions on non-Windows systems are set in a way that disallows the reading of files or certain directories. If the `doc/` directory or files in it cannot be accessed by TYPO3 Extension Manager, they will not be uploaded to TER. If the directory is accessible for reading but the file is not, then the file will be uploaded with zero length causing the **Manual cannot be rendered** error in TER.

Always check file system permissions before sending extensions to TER.

Uploading Extensions to TER

An extension is uploaded to the TYPO3 Extension Repository using the Extension Manager. Click on the extension name in the Extension Manager and choose **Upload to TER** from the function menu.

When an extension is uploaded to TER, the developer should specify a comment. As usual, respect your users and provide a good comment that tells the users what the changes were. It is not worth pasting the full change log if it is too long (you have it in the ChangeLog file already). But outlining the most important changes is always a good thing to do.

Another important question is about extension versioning.

TYPO3 follows the PHP versioning scheme. This means that there are three version numbers. The first number changes when something major is introduced, or the product is remade completely. When this happens, the remaining numbers are set to zero.

The second number changes when a certain feature is introduced, or a major bug is fixed, or lots of bugs are fixed.

The third number is changed for small bug fix releases.

Why is this important to know?

There are lots of extensions in the TYPO3 repository that have version numbers similar to 0.64.39 or so. It usually means that the author is simply afraid of declaring a major release of the product. This is a typical problem of open source software – a product exists for years, but never gets major release (version 1.0). One of my favorite examples is eAccelerator, which is a great accelerator for PHP. At the time of writing this book, the version number was 0.9.5.4. And this product has been in development for more than two years, and is installed in thousands of web servers across the world! Another example is Wine. Wine is a Windows emulator for Linux. It was used for 15 years before the version 1.0.0 was released.

When an extension fulfills all the declared requirements, its version number should be set to 1.0.0. Do not be afraid. Everyone makes mistakes, and every software has bugs. There is no such thing as a perfect software. Declare your extension as 1.0.0 and increase its version number as you fix the bugs. Let your users know that the version is stable in terms of functionality, and you are fixing bugs. This is the right thing to do.

Summary

This chapter was the last chapter of the book. We started the book with the overview of TYPO3 Core API, walked through extension generation and code writing until uploading the extension to TER. It was a long way. This chapter adds the final polish to your extension. Good luck to the reader of this book in writing spectacular extensions. The author of the book truly expects better and better extensions coming from you into TER soon!

Index

Printed in the United States
126786LV00003B/144/P